Collins

Unlocking FRENCH

with

Paul Noble

Published by Collins
An imprint of HarperCollins Publishers
Westerhill Road
Bishopbriggs
Glasgow G64 2QT

HarperCollins Publishers
1st Floor, Watermarque Building
Ringsend Road, Dublin 4, Ireland

First edition 2017

10 9 8 7 6

© Paul Noble 2017

ISBN 978-0-00-813586-7
US ISBN 978-0-00-854722-6

Collins® is a registered trademark of
HarperCollins Publishers Limited

Typeset by Davidson Publishing Solutions,
Glasgow

Printed in Italy by Grafica Veneta S.p.A.

All rights reserved. No part of this book may
be reproduced, stored in a retrieval system,
or transmitted in any form of by any means,
electronic, mechanical, photocopying,
recording or otherwise, without the prior
permission in writing of the Publisher. This
book is sold subject to the conditions that
it shall not, by way of trade or otherwise,
be lent, re-sold, hired out or otherwise
circulated without the Publisher's prior
consent in any form of binding or cover
other than that in which it is published and
without a similar condition including this
condition being imposed on the subsequent
purchaser.

Entered words that we have reason to
believe constitute trademarks have been
designated as such. However, neither the
presence nor absence of such designation
should be regarded as affecting the legal
status of any trademark.

The contents of this publication are believed
correct at the time of printing. Nevertheless
the Publisher can accept no responsibility
for errors or omissions, changes in the detail
given or for any expense or loss thereby
caused.

HarperCollins does not warrant that any
website mentioned in this title will be
provided uninterrupted, than any website
will be error free, that defects will be
corrected, or that the website or the server
that makes it available are free of viruses or
bugs. For full terms and conditions please
refer to the site terms provided on the website.

A catalogue record for this book is available
from the British Library.

If you would like to comment on any aspect
of this book, please contact us at the given
address or online.
E-mail dictionaries@harpercollins.co.uk
 www.facebook.com/collinsdictionary
 @collinsdict

Acknowledgements
Images from Shutterstock.

MANAGING EDITOR
Maree Airlie

CONTRIBUTORS
Alice Grandison
Jennifer Baird
Laurence Larroche

FOR THE PUBLISHER
Gerry Breslin
Holly Tarbet
Kevin Robbins
Vaila Donnachie

MIX
Paper from
responsible sources
FSC™ C007454

This book is produced from independently certified FSC™ paper
to ensure responsible forest management.

For more information visit: www.harpercollins.co.uk/green

People who know no French at all

People who know some French already

People who studied French at school

People who didn't study French at school

People who didn't like how languages were taught at school

*People who are amazed by just how closely grammar
books resemble furniture assembly instructions*

Who is this book for?

People who think they can't learn a foreign language

People who've listened to one of Paul Noble's audio courses

People who haven't listened to one of Paul Noble's audio courses

People learning French for the first time

People coming back to the language after a break

People curious about whether they can learn a language

**People who feel confused by the way languages
are normally taught**

Contents

Did you know you
already speak French?

Did you know you already speak French?

Did you know you already speak French? That you speak it every day? That you read and write it every day? That you use it with your friends, with your family, at work, down the post office – even in the shower when you read the label on the shampoo bottle?

Were you aware of that fact?

Well, even if you weren't, it's nevertheless true.

Of course, you might not have realised at the time that what you were reading / saying / writing was actually French but I can prove to you that it was. Just take a look at these words below:

important	conversation	table	dessert
impossible	simple	invisible	noble
prison	urgent	attitude	patience

concert	terrible	club	normal
restaurant	courage	excellent	signature
intelligent	probable		

Have you read through them?
yes? Good.

Now, answer me this, are they:

A: English words
B: French words
C: Both

Well, if you're reading this book then you're clearly already a highly intelligent person with good judgement, so you will have correctly chosen "C".

Yes, these are words that we have in English *but* they have come into English from French and they are, of course, still in use in French today. And these are by no means isolated examples of French words in English but rather they are merely the tip of a *truly enormous* iceberg.

In fact, around half of all English words have come into our language via French. Yes, that's right, **half!**

If we begin using these words, together with an extremely subtle method that shows you how to put them into sentences in a way that's almost effortless, then becoming a competent French speaker becomes really quite easy.

The only thing that *you* will need to do to make this happen is to follow the three simple rules printed on the following pages. These rules will explain to you how to use this book so that you can begin unlocking the French language for yourself in a matter of hours.

Well, what are you waiting for? Turn the page!

Rule Number 1:

Don't skip anything!

Using this book is extremely simple – and highly effective – *if* you follow its three simple rules.

If you don't want to follow them, then I recommend that, instead of reading the book, you use it to prop up a wobbly coffee table, as it won't work if you don't follow the rules. Now get ready – because here's the first one!

Each and every little thing in this book has been put where it is, in a very particular order, for a very particular reason. So, if the book asks you to read or do something, then do it! Who's the teacher after all, you or me, eh?

Also, each part of the book builds on and reinforces what came before it. If you start skipping sections, you will end up confused and lost. Instead, you should just take your time and gently work your way through the book at your own pace – *but without skipping anything!*

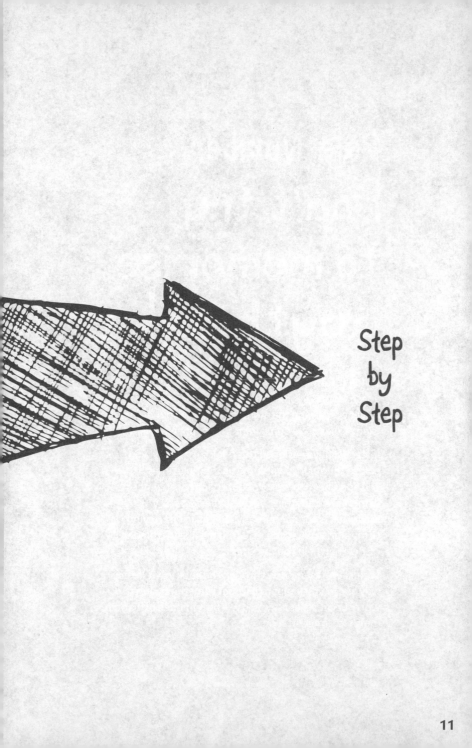

Step
by
Step

Rule Number 2:
Don't try to memorise anything!

Trying to jam things into your head is boring *and* it doesn't work. People often cram for tests and then forget everything the moment they walk out of the exam. Clearly, we don't want that happening here.

Instead, I have designed this book so that any word or idea taught in it will come up multiple times. You don't need to worry about trying to remember or memorise anything because the necessary repetition is actually already built in. In fact, trying to memorise what you're learning is likely to hinder rather than help your progress.

So, just work your way through the book in a relaxed way and, if you happen to forget something, don't worry because, as I say, you will be reminded of it again, multiple times, later on.

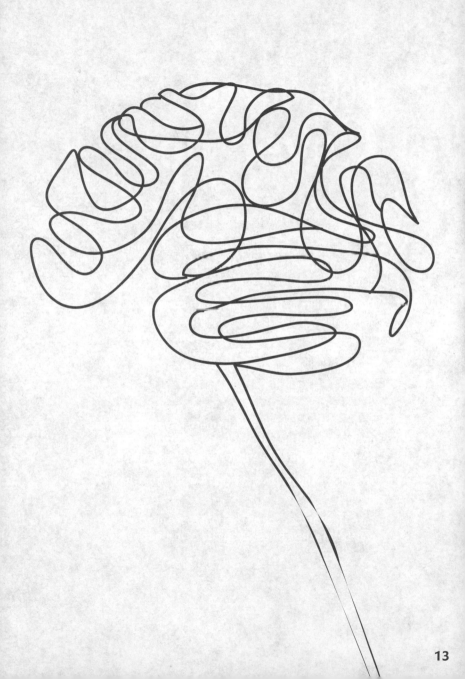

Rule Number 3:
Cover up!

No, I'm not being a puritan grandmother and telling you to put on a long-sleeved cardigan. Instead, I'm asking you to take a bookmark or piece of paper and use it to cover up any **blue text** that you come across as you work your way through the book.

These **blue bits** are the answers to the various riddles, challenges and questions that I will pose as I lead you into the French language. If you read these answers without at least trying to work out the solutions first, then the book simply won't work for you.

So, make sure to use something to cover up the bits of **blue text** in the book while you have a go at trying to work out the answers. It doesn't matter if you sometimes get them wrong because it is by trying to think out the answers that you will learn how to use the language.

Trust me on this, you will see that it works from the very first page!

Take a look at the page on the right to see how to use your bookmark or piece of paper to cover up correctly.

I want you to try to say "I visited Paris", bearing in mind that what you're going to say is *exactly* the same as what you just said for "I have visited Paris". So, "I visited Paris" will be:

J'ai visité Paris.
(zhay visit-ay pa-ree)

As you can see, it is exactly the same. The French do not make a distinction between the two. Effectively, you have got two English past tenses for the price of one. And actually it is even better than that.

You can now already correctly say "I have visited Paris" and "I visited Paris" because they are exactly the same in French. With this in mind, do you think you can make a lucky guess about how you might say "I *did* visit Paris"? Just take a wild guess!

J'ai visité Paris.
(zhay visit-ay pa-ree)

Once again, it is exactly the same in French. "I have visited Paris", "I visited Paris" and "I did visit Paris" are all said in precisely the same way. In fact this is one of the many wonderful things about French. You get three English past tenses for the price of one in French. "I have visited Paris", "I visited Paris" and "I did visit Paris" are all simply:

J'ai visité Paris.
(zhay visit-ay pa-ree)

Let's try this 3 for the price of 1 Special Offer again now but this time with a different example.

To say "I have spent" in French, you will literally say "I have passed", which in French is:

J'ai passé
(zhay pass-ay)

"The weekend" in French is:

le week-end
(luh weekend)

So how would you say "I have spent the weekend" (literally "I have passed the weekend")?

J'ai passé le week-end
(zhay pass-ay luh weekend)

And how would you say simply "I spent the weekend" / "I passed the weekend"?

J'ai passé le week-end
(zhay pass-ay luh weekend)

Just as "I visited Paris" and "I have visited Paris" are no different from one another in French, so "I spent the weekend" and "I have spent the weekend" are also no different from one another.

How do you think you would say "I *did* spend the weekend"?

J'ai passé le week-end

Make sure to cover up any blue words, just like this!

à Paris
(a pa-ree)

So how would you say "I have spent the weekend in Paris"?

J'ai passé le week-end à Paris
(zhay pass-ay luh weekend a pa-ree)

And how would you say "I spent the weekend in Paris"?

J'ai passé le week-end à Paris.
(zhay pass-ay luh weekend a pa-ree)

I want you to try to say "I visited Paris", bearing in mind that what you're going to say is *exactly* the same as what you just said for "I have visited Paris". So, "I visited Paris" will be:

J'ai visité Paris.
(zhay visit-ay pa-ree)

As you can see, it is exactly the same. The French do not make a distinction between the two. Effectively, you have got two English past tenses for the price of one. And actually it is even better than that.

You can now already correctly say "I have visited Paris" and "I visited Paris" because they are exactly the same in French. With this in mind, do you think you can make a lucky guess about how you might say "I *did* visit Paris"? Just take a wild guess!

J'ai visité Paris.
(zhay visit-ay pa-ree)

Once again, it is exactly the same in French. "I have visited Paris", "I visited Paris" and "I did visit Paris" are all said in precisely the same way. In fact this is one of the many wonderful things about French. You get three English past tenses for the price of one in French. "I have visited Paris", "I visited Paris" and "I did visit Paris" are all simply:

J'ai visité Paris.
(zhay visit-ay pa-ree)

Let's try this 3 for the price of 1 Special Offer again now but this time with a different example.

To say "I have spent" in French, you will literally say "I have passed", which in French is:

J'ai passé
(zhay pass-ay)

"The weekend" in French is:

le week-end
(luh weekend)

So how would you say "I have spent the weekend" (literally "I have passed the weekend")?

J'ai passé le week-end
(zhay pass-ay luh weekend)

And how would you say simply "I spent the weekend" / "I passed the weekend"?

J'ai passé le week-end
(zhay pass-ay luh weekend)

Just as "I visited Paris" and "I have visited Paris" are no different from one another in French, so "I spent the weekend" and "I have spent the weekend" are also no different from one another.

How do you think you would say "I *did* spend the weekend"?

J'ai passé le week-end
(zhay pass-ay luh weekend)

Then, having tried to work out the answer, uncover and check!

So how would you say "I have spent the weekend in Paris"?

J'ai passé le week-end à Paris
(zhay pass-ay luh weekend a pa-ree)

And how would you say "I spent the weekend in Paris"?

J'ai passé le week-end à Paris.
(zhay pass-ay luh weekend a pa-ree)

20

21

CHAPTER 1

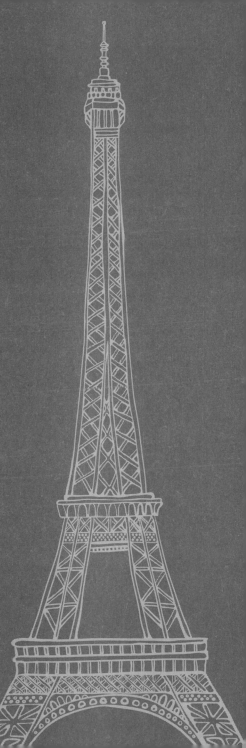

I spent the
weekend in
Paris...
and it
was lovely

> **"I spent the weekend in Paris... and it was lovely."**
> **Not such a complicated sentence in English, is it?**
> **Or is it...?**

I have taught many people over the years, ranging from those who know no French at all, through to those who may have studied French for several years at school. Yet whether they have studied the language before or not, almost none of them tend to be able to construct a basic sentence like this when I first meet them.

Admittedly, they might know how to say other far less useful things, like: "I'm 37 years old and have two sisters and a goldfish" – an unusual conversation opener from my perspective – but they can't say what they did at the weekend.

Well, in just a few minutes' time, you *will* be able to do this – even if you've never learnt any French before.

Just remember though: ***don't* skip anything, *don't* waste your time trying to memorise anything but *do* use your book mark to cover up anything blue you find on each page.**

Okay now, let's begin!

"I have" in French is:
J'ai
(pronounced "zhay"[1])

And the word for "visited" in French is:
visité
(pronounced "visit-ay")

With this in mind, how would you say "I have visited"?

J'ai visité
(zhay visit-ay) ◄——— Did you remember to cover up the blue words while you worked out the answer?

---

1   Here's a bit of extra pronunciation guidance for you: the letter "j" in French is pronounced like the "s" in the middle of the English words "pleasure" and "leisure". I have written this sound as a "zh" in the pronunciation guide (given underneath each French word in the book). This means that the whole word "j'ai" ends up sounding like "zhay". Try saying "pleasure" or "leisure" out loud and you'll soon get used to this "zh" sound which is used a lot in French.

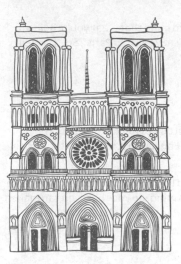

You will almost certainly have heard of the famous cathedral "Notre-Dame" in Paris. So, how do you think you would say "I have visited Notre-Dame"?

J'ai visité Notre-Dame.
(zhay visit-ay not-ruh darm)

The word "Paris" in French is pronounced "pa-ree".

Bearing this pronunciation in mind, how would you say "I have visited Paris"?

J'ai visité Paris.
(zhay visit-ay pa-ree)

Now, if I were to ask you how you would say simply "I visited Paris" rather than "I *have* visited Paris" you might not think you knew how to say that yet. However, you will be glad to hear that I disagree with you because, in French, talking about what has happened in the past is far easier than it is in English. This is because "I visited Paris" and "I have visited Paris" are said in *exactly the same way* in French. I'll show you what I mean.

Again, how do you say "I have visited Paris"?

J'ai visité Paris.
(zhay visit-ay pa-ree)

I want you to try to say "I visited Paris", bearing in mind that what you're going to say is *exactly* the same as what you just said for "I have visited Paris". So, "I visited Paris" will be:

J'ai visité Paris.
(zhay visit-ay pa-ree)

As you can see, it is exactly the same. The French do not make a distinction between the two. Effectively, you have got two English past tenses for the price of one. And actually it is even better than that.

You can now already correctly say "I have visited Paris" and "I visited Paris" because they are exactly the same in French. With this in mind, do you think you can make a lucky guess about how you might say "I *did* visit Paris"? Just take a wild guess!

J'ai visité Paris.
(zhay visit-ay pa-ree)

Once again, it is exactly the same in French. "I have visited Paris", "I visited Paris" and "I did visit Paris" are all said in precisely the same way. In fact this is one of the many wonderful things about French. You get three English past tenses for the price of one in French. "I have visited Paris", "I visited Paris" and "I did visit Paris" are all simply:

J'ai visité Paris.
(zhay visit-ay pa-ree)

Let's try this 3 for the price of 1 Special Offer again now but this time with a different example.

To say "I have spent" in French, you will literally say "I have passed", which in French is:

J'ai passé
(zhay pass-ay)

"The weekend" in French is:

le week-end
(luh weekend)

So how would you say "I have spent the weekend" (literally "I have passed the weekend")?

J'ai passé le week-end
(zhay pass-ay luh weekend)

And how would you say simply "I spent the weekend" / "I passed the weekend"?

J'ai passé le week-end
(zhay pass-ay luh weekend)

Just as "I visited Paris" and "I have visited Paris" are no different from one another in French, so "I spent the weekend" and "I have spent the weekend" are also no different from one another.

How do you think you would you say "I *did* spend the weekend"?

J'ai passé le week-end
(zhay pass-ay luh weekend)

Again, you have three English past tenses for the price of one in French.

"I spent the weekend", "I have spent the weekend",
"I did spend the weekend" – it's all the same in French:
"J'ai passé le week-end".

"In Paris" in French is:

à Paris
(a pa-ree)

So how would you say "I have spent the weekend in Paris"?

J'ai passé le week-end à Paris.
(zhay pass-ay luh weekend a pa-ree)

And how would you say "I spent the weekend in Paris"?

J'ai passé le week-end à Paris.
(zhay pass-ay luh weekend a pa-ree)

And "I did spend the weekend in Paris"?

J'ai passé le week-end à Paris.
(zhay pass-ay luh weekend a pa-ree)

Time to steal some words!
Word Robbery Number 1

Let's forget our weekend in Paris for just one moment now and start stealing some words. Around half the words in modern English have come into our language via French. Once you can identify them, you will have a large, instant, usable vocabulary in French. After all, why bother learning French vocabulary when you can simply steal it?

The first group of words we are going to steal are words that end in "**ic**" and "**ical**" in English.

Words like "romant**ic**", "exot**ic**", "illog**ical**", "typ**ical**" and so on.

There are around 750 of these in English and they are the same in French, except that in French they end in "**ique**" (pronounced "eek"), becoming "romant**ique**", "exot**ique**", "illog**ique**", "typ**ique**" and so on.

Let's now see how we can work these into our weekend in Paris and expand our range of expressions in French!

Words stolen so far 750

Bearing in mind what we've just learnt in the Word Robbery above, let's try changing the "**ic**" on the end of the English word "romant**ic**" into "**ique**".

Doing this, what will "romantic" be in French?

romantique
(roe-mon-teek)

And so what will "fantastic" be in French?

fantastique
(fon-tass-teek)

Let's now try doing the same with "**ical**". Change the "**ical**" on the end of "typ**ical**" into "**ique**".

Doing this, what will "typical" be in French?

typique
(tip-eek)

And what will "political" be?

politique
(po-lee-teek)

Let's now try using these "ique" words to expand our range of expressions and to make some more complex sentences in French.

"It was" in French is:

C'était
(set-ay)

So, how would you say "it was political"?

C'était politique.
(set-ay po-lee-teek)

And how would you say "it was typical"?

C'était typique.
(set-ay tip-eek)

How about "it was romantic"?

C'était romantique.
(set-ay roe-mon-teek)

Finally, how would you say "it was fantastic"?

C'était fantastique.
(set-ay fon-tass-teek)

Now, do you remember how to say "I have visited" in French?

J'ai visité
(zhay visit-ay)

And what about "I visited"?

J'ai visité
(zhay visit-ay)

And "I did visit"?

J'ai visité
(zhay visit-ay)

Do you remember how to say "I have spent", "I did spend", "I spent"
(literally "I have passed")?

J'ai passé
(zhay pass-ay)

And how would you say "I spent the weekend"?

J'ai passé le week-end
(zhay pass-ay luh weekend)

And how do you say "in Paris" in French?

à Paris
(a pa-ree)

So how would you say "I spent the weekend in Paris"?

J'ai passé le week-end à Paris.
(zhay pass-ay luh weekend a pa-ree)

And once more, what was "fantastic" in French?

fantastique
(fon-tass-teek)

And do you remember how to say "it was"?

c'était
(set-ay)

So, how would you say "it was fantastic"?

C'était fantastique.
(set-ay fon-tass-teek)

The word for "and" in French is:

et
(ay)

So, how would you say "…and it was fantastic"?

…et c'était fantastique
(ay set-ay fon-tass-teek)

Putting what you've learnt together, say "I spent the weekend in Paris and it was fantastic." Take your time to work this out, bit by bit, there's no rush.

J'ai passé le week-end à Paris… et c'était fantastique.
(zhay pass-ay luh weekend a pa-ree… ay set-ay fon-tass-teek)

Of course, perhaps you would prefer to describe your weekend in a different way. Perhaps it was more "lovely" than it was "fantastic", so let's try that. The French might express the idea that such a weekend was "lovely" by saying that it had been "very agreeable".

"Very agreeable" in French is:

très agréable
(trez ag-ray-arb-luh)

So, how would you say "it was very agreeable" / "it was lovely" in French?

C'était très agréable.
(set-ay trez ag-ray-arb-luh)

Finally, how would you say "I spent the weekend in Paris… and it was lovely"?

J'ai passé le week-end à Paris… et c'était très agréable.
(zhay pass-ay luh weekend a pa-ree… ay set-ay trez ag-ray-arb-luh)

You can now construct the sentence with which we started the chapter – and, as you will soon discover, this is just the very beginning of your journey into French!

Building Blocks

You just learnt how to say (amongst other things) "I spent the weekend in Paris… and it was lovely".

Now that you can do this, you are going to move on to expanding what you can say through the use of additional "building blocks".

The new building blocks you are going to learn will allow you to begin instantly expanding your range of expressions in the French language.

So far, some of the building blocks you have already learnt include:

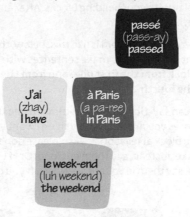

passé
(pass-ay)
passed

J'ai
(zhay)
I have

à Paris
(a pa-ree)
in Paris

le week-end
(luh weekend)
the weekend

You already know how to use these building blocks to construct a sentence. Once again, how would you say "I have spent the weekend in Paris"?

J'ai
(zhay)

passé
(pass-ay)

le week-end
(luh weekend)

à Paris
(a pa-ree)

As you can see, you already know how to build the four building blocks above into a sentence. Take a look now at the six new building blocks below. Just have a glance over them and then I'll show you how you're going to add these into the mix of what you've learnt so far.

Nous avons
(noo za-von)
We have

Vous avez
(voo za-vay)
You have

en France
(on fronce)
in France

Noël
(no-ell)
Christmas

septembre
(sep-tom-bruh)
September

en Suisse
(on swees)
in Switzerland

Okay, first things first: please don't try to memorise them. No, no, no! Instead, I simply want you to play with your building blocks. After all, that's what building blocks are for, isn't it?

The way you're going to play with them is like this: below, they have been put in four piles and all I want you to do is to make sentences with them. **You'll do this by using one building block from the first pile, one from the second, one from the third and one from the fourth.**

You will find that you can say a lot of different things using them in this way and it's up to you what sentences you make. The only thing I want you to make sure you do is to use every building block at least once. Also, please don't bother writing down the sentences you make. Instead, say them out loud. Or, if you're not in a place where you can do this, say them in your head. Now, off you go – make as many sentences as you can!

* Remember, of course, that "J'ai passé" means "I have spent", "I spent" and "I did spend". And this means, of course, that "vous avez passé" means "you have spent", "you spent" and "you did spend". And therefore "nous avons passé" means not only "we have spent" but also "we spent" and "we did spend". Don't forget, you get three English past tenses for the price of one in French and this applies whether you're saying "I...", "you...", "we..." or whatever.

The Checklist

You have now reached the final part of the first chapter. Once you have finished this short section you will not only have completed your first chapter but you will also understand how this book works. All the other chapters follow the same pattern, with your French becoming ever more sophisticated as you complete each chapter.

The section you are now on will be the final part of each chapter and is what I call "The Checklist". It involves nothing more than a read-through of a selection of the words or expressions you have so far encountered.

You will actually see The Checklist twice. The first time you will see that the French words are written in **black** (on the left-hand side) and that the English words are written in blue (on the right-hand side) – and you know what blue means… cover up!

So, what I want you to do here is to cover up the English words (which are written in blue on the right-hand side) while you read through the list of French words on the left. Read through them all, from the top of the list to the bottom, and see if you can recall what they mean in English (uncover one blue word at a time to check if you've remembered the meaning correctly). If you can go through the entire list, giving the correct English meaning for each of the French words / expressions **without making more than three mistakes in total**, then you're done. If not, then go through the list again. Keep doing this, either working from the top of the list to the bottom or from the bottom to the top (it doesn't matter which) until you can do it **without making more than three mistakes**.

Got it? Then let's go!

le week-end (luh weekend)	the weekend
romantique (roe-mon-teek)	romantic
fantastique (fon-tass-teek)	fantastic
typique (tip-eek)	typical
politique (po-lee-teek)	political
J'ai (zhay)	I have
visité (visit-ay)	visited
J'ai visité (zhay visit-ay)	I have visited / I visited / I did visit
Paris (pa-ree)	Paris
Notre-Dame (not-re darm)	Notre-Dame

J'ai visité Notre-Dame. (zhay visit-ay not-re darm)	I have visited Notre-Dame / I visited Notre-Dame / I did visit Notre-Dame.
passé (pass-ay)	spent
J'ai passé (zhay pass-ay)	I have spent / I spent / I did spend
Vous avez (voo za-vay)	You have
Vous avez passé (voo za-vay pass-ay)	You have spent / You spent / You did spend
Nous avons (noo za-von)	We have
Nous avons passé (noo za-von pass-ay)	We have spent / We spent / We did spend
septembre (sep-tom-bruh)	September
Noël (no-ell)	Christmas
à Paris (a pa-ree)	in Paris
en France (on fronce)	in France
en Suisse (on swees)	in Switzerland
Nous avons passé Noël en Suisse. (noo za-von pass-ay no-ell on swees)	We spent Christmas in Switzerland.
Vous avez passé septembre en France. (voo za-vay pass-ay sep-tom-bruh on fronce)	You spent September in France.
et (ay)	and
c'était (set-ay)	it was
C'était fantastique. (set-ay fon-tass-teek)	It was fantastic.
très agréable (trez ag-ray-arb-luh)	lovely / very agreeable
C'était très agréable. (set-ay trez ag-ray-arb-luh)	It was lovely / It was very agreeable.
J'ai passé le week-end à Paris… et c'était très agréable. (zhay pass-ay luh weekend a pa-ree ay set-ay trez ag-ray-arb-luh)	I spent the weekend in Paris… and it was lovely.

Finished working through that checklist and made fewer than three mistakes? Yes? Wonderful!

As that's the case, what I now want you to do is repeat exactly the same process with the checklist below, except that this time you'll be reading through the *English* and trying to recall the French. You'll be doing it the other way round. Just relax and work your way up and down the list until you can give the correct French translation for each of the English words / expressions **again without making more than three mistakes in total**. It's not a competition – and I'm not asking you to memorise them. Just look at the English words (on the left-hand side) while you cover up the blue French words on the right-hand side and see if you can remember how to say them in French. You'll be surprised by how many you get right, even on the first try.

Okay, off you go!

the weekend	**le week-end** (luh weekend)
romantic	**romantique** (roe-mon-teek)
fantastic	**fantastique** (fon-tass-teek)
typical	**typique** (tip-eek)
political	**politique** (po-lee-teek)
I have	**J'ai** (zhay)
visited	**visité** (visit-ay)
I have visited / I visited / I did visit	**J'ai visité** (zhay visit-ay)
Paris	**Paris** (pa-ree)
Notre-Dame	**Notre-Dame** (not-re darm)
I have visited Notre-Dame / I visited Notre-Dame / I did visit Notre-Dame.	**J'ai visité Notre-Dame.** (zhay visit-ay not-re darm)
spent	**passé** (pass-ay)
I have spent / I spent / I did spend	**J'ai passé** (zhay pass-ay)
You have	**Vous avez** (voo za-vay)
You have spent / You spent / You did spend	**Vous avez passé** (voo za-vay pass-ay)
We have	**Nous avons** (noo za-von)
We have spent / We spent / We did spend	**Nous avons passé** (noo za-von pass-ay)
September	**septembre** (sep-tom-bruh)
Christmas	**Noël** (no-ell)
in Paris	**à Paris** (a pa-ree)

in France	**en France** (on fronce)
in Switzerland	**en Suisse** (on swees)
We spent Christmas in Switzerland.	**Nous avons passé Noël en Suisse.** (noo za-von pass-ay no-ell on swees)
You spent September in France.	**Vous avez passé septembre en France.** (voo za-vay pass-ay sep-tom-bruh on fronce)
and	**et** (ay)
it was	**c'était** (set-ay)
It was fantastic.	**C'était fantastique.** (set-ay fon-tass-teek)
lovely / very agreeable	**très agréable** (trez ag-ray-arb-luh)
It was lovely. / It was very agreeable.	**C'était très agréable.** (set-ay trez ag-ray-arb-luh)
I spent the weekend in Paris… and it was lovely.	**J'ai passé le week-end à Paris… et c'était très agréable.** (zhay pass-ay luh weekend a pa-ree ay set-ay trez ag-ray-arb-luh)

Well, that's it, you're done with Chapter 1! Don't forget, you mustn't try to hold onto or remember anything you've learnt here. Anything you learn in earlier chapters will be brought up again and reinforced in later chapters. You don't need to do extra work or make any effort to memorise anything. The book has been organised to do that for you. Off you go now and have a rest. You've earned it!

Between Chapters Tip!

Between chapters, I'm going to be giving you various tips on language learning. These will range from useful tips about the French language itself to advice on how to fit learning a language into your daily routine. Ready for the first one? Here it is!

Learning a language is like building a fire – if you don't tend to it, it will go out. So, once you have decided to learn a foreign language, you really should study it every day.

It doesn't have to be for a long time though. Just five or ten minutes each day will be enough, so long as you keep it up. Doing these five or ten minutes will stop you forgetting what you've already learnt and, over time, will let you put more meat on the bones of what you're learning.

As for what counts towards those five or ten minutes – well, that's up to you. Whilst you're working with this book, I would recommend that your five or ten minutes should be spent here learning with me. Once you're done here, however, your daily study could be spent reading a French newspaper, watching a French film, or chatting with a French-speaking acquaintance. You could even attend a class if you want to learn in a more formal setting. The important thing is to make sure that you do a little every day.

CHAPTER 2

I booked a table, ordered dinner
and then paid the bill.
What did you do?

> I booked a table, ordered dinner and then paid the bill. What did you do?

The first chapter has shown you that you can learn how to create full and complex sentences in French with relative ease. It also began to show you how to convert huge numbers of English words into French and then start using them straight away.

We will be doing more of both here, which will allow you to make enormous strides with your French in an incredibly short space of time.

Let's begin by carrying out a second Word Robbery…

Time to steal some words!
Word Robbery Number 2

The second group of words we are going to steal are words that end in "**ion**" in English.

Words such as:

accusation   reservation   decoration   invitation   confirmation cooperation   imagination   irritation   manipulation   perfection domination   creation   innovation   inspiration   donation   association concentration   anticipation   information   exploration   occupation

There are around 1250 of these in English and we can begin using these in French right now.

Adding them to the words we've already stolen so far, we have now reached a total of 2000 words stolen – and we're only on Chapter 2!

Words stolen so far 2000

We've now carried out our second Word Robbery and have gained more than a thousand words ending in "ion", and it only took us thirty seconds to "learn" them.

If you look at the examples above, you'll notice that most, though not all, of these "ion" words actually end in "ation".

When they do, they become even more useful because you can then use them to make the past tense in French.

Let me show you how.

Let's take "réservation" as an example.

The first thing you're going to do with "réservation" is to cut off the "ation" at the end. Do this now and tell me, what are you left with?

réserv
(ray-zurv)

Good. Now, onto the end of this, I want you to add the "é" that you find on the end of the word "café". So again, I simply want you to take "réserv" and add an "é" onto the end of it.

What word does that give you?

réservé
(ray-zurv-ay)

This means "reserved". (And notice, from the pronunciation guide underneath "réservé", that "é" is always pronounced "ay" in French).

Let's try doing this again, this time with the word "invitation". Once more, cut off the "ation" from the end of the word and replace it with the "é" you find at the end of the word "café".

Doing this, what do you get?

invité
(earn-vit-ay)

This means "invited".

Let's try this one more time, as the more practice you get, the easier it will become.

Take the word "prépar ation" as the starting point this time. Again, cut off the " ation" from the end and add an " é" in its place.

What does that give you?

préparé
(pray-par-ay)

This means "prepared".

Now again, what was "I have" in French?

J'ai
(zhay)

So, how would you say "I have prepared"?

J'ai préparé
(zhay pray-par-ay)

And "I prepared"?

J'ai préparé
(zhay pray-par-ay)

And "I did prepare"?

J'ai préparé
(zhay pray-par-ay)

(Once again, just in case you'd forgotten, you get three English past tenses for the price of one in French!)

"The dinner" in French is:

le dîner
(luh din-ay)

How would you say "I have prepared the dinner", "I prepared the dinner", "I did prepare the dinner"?

J'ai préparé le dîner.
(zhay pray-par-ay luh din-ay)

Alright, let's return again to our 1200 " ation" words for a moment.

Once more, what was "reservation" in French?

réservation
(ray-zurv-ass-yon)

As before, let's cut the " ation" off the end of "réserv ation" and replace it with the " é" from "caf é" to create the word that means "reserved" in French.

If you do that, what is "reserved"?

réservé
(ray-zurv-ay)

And this actually means both "reserved" and "booked". So, how would you say, "I have reserved" / "I have booked"?

J'ai réservé
(zhay ray-zurv-ay)

"A table" in French is

une table
(oon tarb-luh)

Right, how would you say "I have reserved a table" / "I have booked a table"?

J'ai réservé une table.
(zhay ray-zurv-ay oon tarb-luh)

"For you" in French is:

pour vous
(poor voo)

How would you say "I have reserved a table for you" / "I have booked a table for you"?

J'ai réservé une table pour vous.
(zhay ray-zurv-ay oon tarb-luh poor voo)

And again, what was "the dinner" in French?

le dîner
(luh din-ay)

And what was "for you"?

pour vous
(poor voo)

So, if "pour vous" means "for you", what do you think is the word for "for" in French?

pour
(poor)

Now, to say "for dinner" in French, you will literally say "for *the* dinner". How do you think you would say that?

pour le dîner
(poor luh din-ay)

Alright, how would you say "I have reserved a table for dinner" / "I have booked a table for dinner"?

J'ai réservé une table pour le dîner.
(zhay ray-zurv-ay oon tarb-luh poor luh din-ay)

As you can see, these "ation" words really are very useful. Not only do you get more than a thousand words right away – like "réservation", "préparation", "information" and so on – for free but these "ation" words also give you access to the past tense in French, allowing you to create many, many new words such as "reserved", "prepared", "informed" and so on. And you can achieve this simply by cutting off the "ation" from the end of the word and and adding an "é" in its place.

Actually there are many other English words you can make into the past tense in French simply by adding the "é" from "café" onto the end of them – and for these you don't even need to cut anything off first!

For example, take the English word "command" and add an "é" onto the end of it. Do that now – what do you get?

commandé
(comm-on-day)

This means "commanded".

Well actually, it doesn't only mean "commanded", it also means "ordered". This makes sense really, if you think about it – after all, an order and a command are more or less the same thing, aren't they?

Now that you know that "commandé" means both "commanded" and "ordered", how would you say "I have ordered", "I ordered", "I did order"?

J'ai *commandé*
(zhay *comm-on-day*)

And how would you say "I ordered dinner" (you will say literally "I *have* ordered *the* dinner")?

J'ai *commandé le dîner.*
(zhay *comm-on-day* luh din-ay)

"The roast beef" in French is:

le rosbif
(luh ros-beef)

So how would you say "I ordered roast beef" (again, you will literally say "I *have* ordered *the* roast beef")?

J'ai *commandé le rosbif.*
(zhay *comm-on-day* luh ros-beef)

And once again, how would you say "for dinner" (literally "for *the* dinner") in French?

pour le dîner
(*poor* luh din-ay)

Now put these two things together and say "I ordered roast beef for dinner" (literally "I *have* ordered *the* roast beef for *the* dinner")?

J'ai *commandé le rosbif pour le dîner.*
(zhay *comm-on-day* luh ros-beef poor luh din-ay)

And how would you say "I ordered the roast beef for you"?

J'ai *commandé le rosbif pour vous.*
(zhay *comm-on-day* luh ros-beef poor voo)

Good, now can you recall how to say "I visited"?

J'ai visité
(zhay visit-ay)

How about "I spent"?

J'ai passé
(zhay pass-ay)

"I reserved" / "I booked"?

J'ai réservé
(zhay ray-zurv-ay)

"I prepared"?

J'ai préparé
(zhay pray-par-ay)

"I ordered"?

J'ai commandé
(zhay comm-on-day)

To say "paid" in French, you can simply take the English word "pay" and once again add an "é" onto the end of it.

Do that now – what do you get?

payé
(pay-ay)

So, how would you say "I paid"?

J'ai payé
(zhay pay-ay)

Do you remember what "we have" is from our Building Blocks section in Chapter 1?

If not, don't worry, it's:

Nous avons
(noo za-von)

With this in mind, how would you say "we have paid", "we paid", "we did pay"?

Nous avons payé
(noo za-von pay-ay)

And do you remember what "you have" is in French?

Vous avez
(voo za-vay)

How would you say "you have paid"?

Vous avez payé
(voo za-vay pay-ay)

"The bill" in French is literally "the addition", which in French is:

l'addition
(la-dis-yon)

So, how would you say "you have paid the bill"?

Vous avez payé l'addition
(voo za-vay pay-ay la-dis-yon)

How about "we have paid the bill"?

Nous avons payé l'addition.
(noo za-von pay-ay la-dis-yon)

And "I have paid the bill"?

J'ai payé l'addition.
(zhay pay-ay la-dis-yon)

Again, how would you say "I booked a table"?

J'ai réservé une table.
(zhay ray-zurv-ay oon tarb-luh)

What about "I ordered the dinner"?

J'ai commandé le dîner.
(zhay comm-on-day luh din-ay)

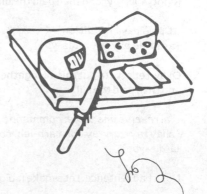

And how about "I paid the bill"?

J'ai payé l'addition.
(zhay pay-ay la-dis-yon)

Let's now try making a list out of these things. Start by
saying "I booked a table, ordered the dinner, paid the bill."
Take your time working it out in your head, bit by bit – there
really is no rush. So again – "I booked a table, ordered the
dinner, paid the bill":

J'ai réservé une table, commandé le dîner, payé l'addition.
(zhay ray-zurv-ay oon tarb-luh, comm-on-day luh din-ay, pay-ay la-dis-yon)

Let's add "then" into this sentence to make it sound more natural. "Then" in
French is:

puis
(pwee)

First try simply saying "then paid the bill". How would you say that?

puis payé l'addition
(pwee pay-ay la-dis-yon)

And what was "and" in French?

et
(ay)

Right, now say "and then paid the bill".

et puis payé l'addition
(ay pwee pay-ay la-dis-yon)

Okay. Let's try to put this all together and say "I booked a table, ordered the dinner
and then paid the bill."

J'ai réservé une table, commandé le dîner et puis payé l'addition.
(zhay ray-zurv-ay oon tarb-luh, comm-on-day luh din-ay ay pwee pay-ay
la-dis-yon)

Not a bad sentence. Let's make it bigger still.

What is "you have" in French?

Vous avez
(*voo* za-vay)

And what is "prepared"?

préparé
(pray-par-ay)

So, how would you say "you have prepared"?

Vous avez préparé
(*voo* za-vay pray-par-ay)

If you want to say "what have you prepared?" in French, one very typical way to express this is to literally say *"what is it that* you have prepared?"

This sounds a bit complex and formal in English, but in French, "what is it that" is a phrase that is used all the time in everyday language and it's very simple to pronounce (though it doesn't necessarily look it!).

"What Is it that" in French is:

Qu'est-ce que
(kess-kuh)

Again, how would you say "you have prepared" in French?

Vous avez préparé
(*voo* za-vay pray-par-ay)

And how would you say "what is it that"?

Qu'est-ce que
(kess-kuh)

To say "what have you prepared?", you can simply say "what is it that you have prepared?" Let's do that now. Again, what is "what is it that?"

Qu'est-ce que
(kess-kuh)

And what is "you have prepared"?

Vous avez préparé
(*voo za-vay pray-par-ay*)

So, how would you say "what is it that you have prepared?"?

Qu'est-ce que vous avez préparé ?
(*kess-kuh voo za-vay pray-par-ay*)

Literally this means "what is it that you have prepared?", but it means not only "what have you prepared?", it also means "what did you prepare?" Just as before, even though it's a question, you still get more than one English past tense for the price of one in French.

Just to make sure you've understood this 100%, how would you say "What have you prepared?"?

Qu'est-ce que vous avez préparé ?
(*kess-kuh voo za-vay pray-par-ay*)

And "what did you prepare"?

Qu'est-ce que vous avez préparé ?
(*kess-kuh voo za-vay pray-par-ay*)

That's right, they're the same!

And how do you think you would say "what have you reserved?" / "what did you reserve?" (literally "what is it that you have reserved?")?

Qu'est-ce que vous avez réservé ?
(*kess-kuh voo za-vay ray-zurv-ay*)

The word for "done" in French is:

fait
(fay)

So, how would you say "what have you done?" / "what did you do?" (literally "what is it that you have done?")?

Qu'est-ce que vous avez fait ?
(kess-kuh voo za-vay fay)

And once more, how would you say "I reserved a table" / "I booked a table"?

J'ai réservé une table.
(zhay ray-zurv-ay oon tarb-luh)

And how would you say "I ordered the dinner"?

J'ai commandé le dîner.
(zhay comm-on-day luh din-ay)

And remind me, what was the word for "then" in French?

puis
(pwee)

And the word for "and"?

et
(ay)

Now say, "and then paid the bill".

et puis payé l'addition
(ay pwee pay-ay la-dis-yon)

Let's put those bits together again and say "I booked a table, ordered the dinner and then paid the bill."

J'ai réservé une table, commandé le dîner et puis payé l'addition.
(zhay ray-zurv-ay oon tarb-luh, comm-on-day luh din-ay ay pwee pay-ay la-dis-yon)

And let's add the final bit onto it all. Again, how would you say "what is it that"?

Qu'est-ce que
(kess-kuh)

Plus, as I mentioned earlier, "you have done" in French is:

vous avez fait
(*voo* za-vay fay)

So, how would you say "what have you done?" / "what did you do?" (literally "what is it that you have done?")?

Qu'est-ce que vous avez fait ?
(kess-kuh *voo* za-vay fay)

Let's combine absolutely everything together now and (taking your time to think it out) say "I booked a table, ordered dinner and then paid the bill. What did you do?"

J'ai réservé une table, commandé le dîner et puis payé l'addition. Qu'est-ce que vous avez fait ?
(zhay ray-zurv-ay *oon* tarb-luh, comm-on-day luh din-ay, ay pwee pay-ay la-dis-yon. kess-kuh *voo* za-vay fay)

How did you find that final, complex sentence? Try it a few more times, even if you've got it right, until you feel comfortable constructing it. Every time you practise building these long sentences, the naturalness and fluidity of your spoken French will improve and your confidence in speaking will get better along with it.

Building Blocks 2

It's time to add some new building blocks to the mix. As before, it will be just six new ones. Here they are:

Elle a
(ell a)
She has

Il a
(eel a)
He has

une chambre
(oon shom-bruh)
a room*

pour deux
personnes
(poor duh
purse-on)
for two (people)

un taxi
(um taxi)
a taxi

pour ce soir
(poor sir swar)
**for this
evening**

* literally "a chamber".

Once more, these new building blocks have been put into four piles. As previously, what I want you to do is to make sentences with them, each time using one building block from the first pile, one from the second, one from the third and one from the fourth. Make as many sentences as you can!

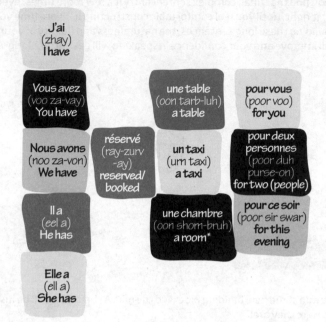

J'ai
(zhay)
I have

Vous avez
(voo za-vay)
You have

une table
(oon tarb-luh)
a table

pour vous
(poor voo)
for you

Nous avons
(noo za-von)
We have

réservé
(ray-zurv
-ay)
reserved/
booked

un taxi
(urn taxi)
a taxi

pour deux
personnes
(poor duh
purse-on)
for two (people)

Il a
(eel a)
He has

une chambre
(oon shom-bruh)
a room*

pour ce soir
(poor sir swar)
for this
evening

Elle a
(ell a)
She has

* literally "a chamber".

Checklist 2

You have now reached your second checklist. Remember, don't skip anything!
The checklists are essential if you want what you've learnt to remain in your
memory for the long term.

So again, cover up the English words on the right-hand side while you read
through the list of French words on the left, trying to recall what they mean in
English. If you can go through the entire list, giving the correct English meaning
for each of the French words / expressions **without making more than three
mistakes in total**, then you're done. If not, then go through the list again. Keep
doing this, either working from the top of the list to the bottom or from the
bottom to the top (it doesn't matter which) until you can do it **without making
more than three mistakes**.

Okay. Ready, set, go!

le week-end (luh weekend)	the weekend
démocratique[2] (day-moe-kra-teek)	democratic
économique (ay-kon-oh-meek)	economic
psychologique (psee-ko-lozh-eek)	psychological
identique (ee-don-teek)	identical
J'ai (zhay)	I have
visité (visit-ay)	visited
J'ai visité (zhay visit-ay)	I have visited / I visited / I did visit
Paris (pa-ree)	Paris
Notre-Dame (not-re darm)	Notre-Dame
J'ai visité Notre-Dame. (zhay visit-ay not-re darm)	I have visited Notre-Dame / I visited Notre-Dame / I did visit Notre-Dame.
passé (pass-ay)	spent
J'ai passé (zhay pass-ay)	I have spent / I spent / I did spend
Vous avez (voo za-vay)	You have
Vous avez passé (voo za-vay pass-ay)	You have spent / You spent / You did spend
Nous avons (noo za-von)	We have
Nous avons passé (noo za-von pass-ay)	We have spent / We spent / We did spend
septembre (sep tom bruh)	September
Noël (no-ell)	Christmas
à Paris (a pa-ree)	in Paris
en France (on fronce)	in France
en Suisse (on swees)	in Switzerland

---

2   You'll notice that the "ic" and "ical" words above are different from the ones I gave you in your previous checklist. This is to give you more variety in practising changing various types of "ic" and "ical" words into "ique". I will do this whenever you learn a conversion technique in one of our Word Robberies so that converting those endings into French becomes second nature for you.

Nous avons passé Noël en Suisse. (noo za-von pass-ay no-ell on swees)	We have spent Christmas in Switzerland / We spent Christmas in Switzerland / We did spend Christmas in Switzerland.
Vous avez passé septembre en France. (voo za-vay pass-ay sep-tom-bruh on fronce)	You have spent September in France / You spent September in France / You did spend September in France.
et (ay)	and
c'était (set-ay)	it was
C'était fantastique. (set-ay fon-tass-teek)	It was fantastic.
très agréable (trez ag-ray-arb-luh)	lovely / very agreeable
C'était très agréable. (set-ay trez ag-ray-arb-luh)	It was lovely. / It was very agreeable.
J'ai passé le week-end à Paris… et c'était très agréable. (zhay pass-ay luh weekend a pa-ree… ay set-ay trez ag-ray-arb-luh)	I spent the weekend in Paris… and it was lovely.
invitation (earn-vit-ass-yon)	invitation
invité (earn-vit-ay)	invited
préparation (pray-par-ass-yon)	preparation
préparé (pray-par-ay)	prepared
réservation (ray-zurv-ass-yon)	reservation
réservé (ray-zurv-ay)	reserved / booked
commandé (comm-on-day)	ordered
payé (pay-ay)	paid
fait (fay)	done
l'addition (la-dis-yon)	the bill
le dîner (luh din-ay)	the dinner
le rosbif (luh ros-beef)	the roast beef
une table (oon tarb-luh)	a table
une chambre (oon shom-bruh)	a room
un taxi (urn taxi)	a taxi

J'ai préparé le dîner. (zhay pray-par-ay luh din-ay)	I have prepared the dinner / I prepared the dinner / I did prepare the dinner.
J'ai commandé le rosbif pour le dîner. (zhay comm-on-day luh ros-beef poor luh din-ay)	I have ordered roast beef for dinner / I ordered roast beef for dinner / I did order roast beef for dinner.
J'ai réservé une table pour vous. (zhay ray-zurv-ay oon tarb-luh poor voo)	I have booked a table for you / I booked a table for you / I did book a table for you.
Elle a (ell a)	She has
Elle a réservé une table pour ce soir. (ell a ray-zurv-ay oon tarb-luh poor sir swar)	She has booked / reserved a table for this evening – She booked / reserved a table for this evening – She did book / reserve a table for this evening.
Il a (eel a)	He has
Il a réservé une chambre pour deux personnes. (eel a ray-zurv-ay oon shom-bruh poor duh purse-on)	He has booked / reserved a room for two people – He booked / reserved a room for two people – He did book / reserve a room for two people.
Nous avons réservé un taxi pour vous. (noo za-von ray-zur-vay urn taxi poor voo)	We have booked a taxi for you / We booked a taxi for you / We did book a taxi for you.
Nous avons payé l'addition. (noo za-von pay-ay la-dis-yon)	We paid the bill / We have paid the the bill / We did pay the bill.
Qu'est-ce que ? (kess-kuh)	What? / What is it that?
Qu'est-ce que vous avez préparé ? (kess-kuh voo za-vay pray-par-ay)	What have you prepared? / What did you prepare? (literally "What is it that you have prepared?")
Qu'est-ce que vous avez fait ? (kess-kuh voo za-vay fay)	What have you done? / What did you do? (literally "What is it that you have done?")
J'ai réservé une table, commandé le dîner et puis payé l'addition. Qu'est-ce que vous avez fait ? (zhay ray-zurv-ay oon tarb-luh, comm-on-day luh din-ay ay pwee pay-ay la-dis-yon. kess-kuh voo za-vay fay)	I booked a table, ordered dinner and then paid the bill. What did you do?

Now, do the same thing once again below, except that this time you'll be reading through the list of English words and trying to recall the French. All you need to do is to be able to do one full read-through of them without making more than three mistakes in total and you're done!

the weekend	le week-end (luh weekend)
democratic	démocratique (day-moe-kra-teek)
economic	économique (ay-kon-oh-meek)
psychological	psychologique (psee-ko-lozh-eek)
identical	identique (ee-don-teek)
I have	J'ai (zhay)
visited	visité (visit-ay)
I have visited / I visited / I did visit	J'ai visité (zhay visit-ay)
Paris	Paris (pa-ree)
Notre-Dame	Notre-Dame (not-re darm)
I have visited Notre-Dame / I visited Notre-Dame / I did visit Notre-Dame.	J'ai visité Notre-Dame. (zhay visit-ay not-re darm)
spent	passé (pass-ay)
I have spent / I spent / I did spend	J'ai passé (zhay pass-ay)
You have	Vous avez (voo za-vay)
You have spent / You spent / You did spend	Vous avez passé (voo za-vay pass-ay)
We have	Nous avons (noo za-von)
We have spent / We spent / We did spend	Nous avons passé (noo za-von pass-ay)
September	septembre (sep-tom-bruh)
Christmas	Noël (no-ell)
in Paris	à Paris (a pa-ree)
in France	en France (on fronce)
in Switzerland	en Suisse (on swees)

We have spent Christmas in Switzerland / We spent Christmas in Switzerland / We did spend Christmas in Switzerland.	Nous avons passé Noël en Suisse. (noo za-von pass-ay no-ell on swees)
You have spent September in France / You spent September in France / You did spend September in France.	Vous avez passé septembre en France. (voo za-vay pass-ay sep-tom-bruh on fronce)
and	et (ay)
it was	c'était (set-ay)
It was fantastic.	C'était fantastique. (set-ay fon-tass-teek)
lovely / very agreeable	très agréable (trez ag-ray-arb-luh)
It was lovely. / It was very agreeable.	C'était très agréable. (set-ay trez ag-ray-arb-luh)
I spent the weekend in Paris… and it was lovely.	J'ai passé le week-end à Paris… et c'était très agréable. (zhay pass-ay luh weekend a pa-ree… ay set-ay trez ag-ray-arb-luh)
invitation	invitation (earn-vit-ass-yon)
invited	invité (earn-vit-ay)
preparation	préparation (pray-par-ass-yon)
prepared	préparé (pray-par-ay)
reservation	réservation (ray-zurv-ass-yon)
reserved / booked	réservé (ray-zurv-ay)
ordered	commandé (comm-on-day)
paid	payé (pay-ay)
done	fait (fay)
the bill	l'addition (la-dis-yon)
the dinner	le dîner (luh din-ay)
the roast beef	le rosbif (luh ros-beef)
a table	une table (oon tarb-luh)
a room	une chambre (oon shom-bruh)
a taxi	un taxi (urn taxi)

I have prepared the dinner / I prepared the dinner / I did prepare the dinner.	J'ai préparé le dîner. (zhay pray-par-ay luh din-ay)
I have ordered roast beef for dinner / I ordered roast beef for dinner / I did order roast beef for dinner.	J'ai commandé le rosbif pour le dîner. (zhay comm-on-day luh ros-beef poor luh din-ay)
I have booked a table for you / I booked a table for you / I did book a table for you.	J'ai réservé une table pour vous. (zhay ray-zurv-ay oon tarb-luh poor voo)
She has	Elle a (ell a)
She has booked / reserved a table for this evening – She booked / reserved a table for this evening – She did book / reserve a table for this evening.	Elle a réservé une table pour ce soir. (ell a ray-zurv-ay oon tarb-luh poor sir swar)
He has	Il a (eel a)
He has booked / reserved a room for two people – He booked / reserved a room for two people – He did book / reserve a room for two people.	Il a réservé une chambre pour deux personnes. (eel a ray-zurv-ay oon shom-bruh poor duh purse-on)
We have booked a taxi for you / We booked a taxi for you / We did book a taxi for you.	Nous avons réservé un taxi pour vous. (noo za-von ray-zur-vay urn taxi poor voo)
We paid the bill / We have paid the the bill / We did pay the bill.	Nous avons payé l'addition. (noo za-von pay-ay la-dis-yon)
What? / What is it that?	Qu'est-ce que ? (kess-kuh)
What have you prepared? / What did you prepare? (literally "What is it that you have prepared?")	Qu'est-ce que vous avez préparé ? (kess-kuh voo za-vay pray-par-ay)
What have you done? / What did you do? (literally "What is it that you have done?")	Qu'est-ce que vous avez fait ? (kess-kuh voo za-vay fay)
I booked a table, ordered dinner and then paid the bill. What did you do?	J'ai réservé une table, commandé le dîner et puis payé l'addition. Qu'est-ce que vous avez fait ? (zhay ray-zurv-ay oon tarb-luh, comm-on-day luh din-ay ay pwee pay-ay la-dis-yon. kess-kuh voo za-vay fay)

Well, that's it, you're done with Chapter 2! Remember, don't try to hold onto anything you've learnt here. Everything you learn in earlier chapters will be brought back up and reinforced in later chapters. You don't need to do anything or make any effort to memorise words. The book has been organised in such a way that it will do that for you. Off you go now and have a rest, please!

Between Chapters Tip!

Stop while you're still enjoying it!

Arnold Schwarzenegger once said that the key to his body-building success was that he stopped his work-out each day just before it started to get boring. On the few occasions he went past that point, he found it incredibly hard to return to the gym again the next day – and he *loved* working out.

As you will almost certainly recall, Tip 1 suggested that you should study every day – which you definitely should do if you can. But that doesn't mean that you should overdo it. So, if you're not really in the mood, just do five minutes. If you are in the mood though, don't push yourself too hard. Stop before you get to the point where it doesn't feel fun any longer. Best to leave yourself feeling hungry for more rather than bloated and fed up!

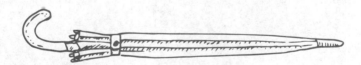

CHAPTER 3

I'm scared of flying, so I'm planning to take the Eurostar.

> # I'm scared of flying, so I'm planning to take the Eurostar.

Person 1: I'm planning to go back to France in May.

Person 2: Really?

Person 1: Yes, I feel like going back to Paris but I'm scared of flying, so I'm planning to take the Eurostar.

The brief conversation above does not seem complicated in English and yet, even if you have studied French before, you might well find it impossible to know exactly where to begin to say all of this in French. By the end of this chapter, you will have learnt how to carry out both sides of this conversation, plus a great deal of other French words and expressions.

Let's begin!

Again, what is "I have" in French?

J'ai
(zhay)

And how would you say "I have visited", "I visited", "I did visit"?

J'ai visité
(zhay visit-ay)

"I have spent", "I spent", "I did spend"?

J'ai passé
(zhay pass-ay)

"I have reserved", "I reserved", "I did reserve"?

J'ai réservé
(zhay ray-zurv-ay)

"I have ordered", "I ordered", "I did order"?

J'ai commandé
(zhay comm-on-day)

"I have prepared", "I prepared", "I did prepare"?

J'ai préparé
(zhay pray-par-ay)

"I have paid", "I paid", "I did pay"?

J'ai payé
(zhay pay-ay)

"I have done", "I did", "I did do"?

J'ai fait
(zhay fay)

So, you definitely know how to use "I have" in French to express a number of things in the past tense.

However, "I have" is not only useful for talking about things that have happened in the past. It also opens up a wide range of extremely useful expressions in French that allow you, for example, to talk about what you're planning to do, feel like doing, or can't stand doing. This is really useful everyday language that will help your French sound natural and colloquial.

Let's start building towards using these expressions now.
"To reserve" or "to book" in French is:

réserver
(ray-zurv-ay[3])

---

3   You may well be saying to yourself, having read the pronunciation guidance below "réserver", "isn't this
     the same way that reserved (réservé) is pronounced?" Well, the answer is "yes"! "To reserve" (réserver) and
     "reserved" (réservé) are pronounced in exactly the same way in French and you'll notice, as you learn more,
     that the same thing happens with many other words in French. This needn't be a cause for concern, as the
     context will make it clear what you mean. For the moment, be aware that, yes, "to reserve" (réserver) and
     "reserved" (réservé) are pronounced in exactly the same way in French (ray-zurv-ay), which fortunately
     means that if you know how to pronounce one then you know how to pronounce the other. Excellent!

Now, what is "a table" in French?

une table
(oon tarb-luh)

So, how would you say "to reserve / to book a table"?

réserver une table
(ray-zurv-ay oon tarb-luh)

And again, what is "I have" in French?

J'ai
(zhay)

"The intention" in French is:

l'intention
(lon-ton-syon)

Alright, how would you say "I have the intention"?

J'ai l'intention
(zhay lon-ton-syon)

The word for "of" in French is:

de
(duh)

So, how would you say "I have the intention of"?

J'ai l'intention de
(zhay lon-ton-syon duh)

Saying "I have the intention of" is actually one way of saying "I'm planning to…" in French.

With this in mind, how would you say "I'm planning to book a table" / "I'm planning to reserve a table" (literally "I have the intention of to reserve a table")?

J'ai l'intention de réserver une table.
(zhay lon-ton-syon duh ray-zurv-ay oon tarb-luh)

Okay, once more, what was "for this evening" in French?

pour ce soir
(poor sir swar)

Now, how would you say "I'm planning to book a table for this evening"
(literally "I have the intention of to reserve a table for this evening")?

J'ai l'intention de réserver une table pour ce soir.
(zhay lon-ton-syon duh ray-zurv-ay oon tarb-luh poor sir swar)

And what was "a room" in French?

une chambre
(oon shom-bruh)

How would you say "I'm planning to book a room for this evening"?

J'ai l'intention de réserver une chambre pour ce soir.
(zhay lon-ton-syon duh ray-zurv-ay oon shom-bruh poor sir swar)

"To go back" in French is literally "to return", which in French is:

retourner
(ruh-toor-nay)

So, how would you say "I'm planning to go back"?

J'ai l'intention de retourner
(zhay lon-ton-syon duh ruh-toor-nay)

And again, how would you say "in France"?

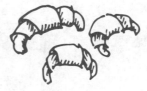

en France
(on fronce)

"To France" is said in *exactly the same way* as
"in France". How would you say "to France"?

en France
(on fronce)

And how would you say "I'm planning to go back (literally "to return") to France"?

J'ai l'intention de retourner en France.
(zhay lon-ton-syon duh ruh-toor-nay on fronce)

"In May" in French is:

en mai
(on mey)

With this in mind, how would you say, "I'm planning to go back to France in May"?

J'ai l'intention de retourner en France en mai.
(zhay lon-ton-syon duh ruh-toor-nay on fronce on mey)

To recap, in French, if you want to say "I'm planning to..." you can simply use "I have the intention of...".

It's an extremely useful expression and actually is just one of a number of such expressions that work in more or less the same way.

For example, if you want to say "I feel like..." or "I fancy..." in French, you will literally say "I have envy of..." which in French is:

J'ai *envie de*
(zhay *on-vee duh*)

Knowing this, how would you say "I feel like going back to France in May / I fancy going back to France in May" (literally "I have envy of to return to France in May")?

J'ai envie de retourner en France en mai.
(zhay on-vee duh ruh-toor-nay on fronce on mey)

What is "September" in French?

septembre
(sep-tom-bruh)

So, how would you say "in September"?

en septembre
(on sep-tom-bruh)

And how would you say "I feel like going back to France in September / I fancy going back to France in September" (literally "I have envy of to return to France in September")?

J'ai envie de retourner en France en septembre.
(zhay on-vee duh ruh-toor-nay on fronce on sep-tom-bruh)

Do you remember how to say "in Paris"?

à Paris
(a pa-ree)

"To Paris" in French is said in exactly the same way – how would you say "to Paris"?

à Paris
(a pa-ree)

And how would you say "I feel like going back to Paris / I fancy going back to Paris"?

J'ai envie de retourner à Paris.
(zhay on-vee duh ruh-toor-nay a pa-ree)

You have now learnt two phrases that are constructed in a similar way. The first uses the words "I have the intention of..." to express "I'm planning to..." and the other uses the words "I have envy of..." to mean "I feel like..." or "I fancy...".

Let's add another one to the mix. But again, don't worry about trying to memorise any of this. As you work your way through the rest of the chapter, you'll find that everything comes up again and again, jolting your memory each time and helping those words and phrases to stick without you having to resort to memorisation or learning by rote. You will be reminded of these things when the time is right.

Now, to say "I'm scared of..." in French, you will literally say "I have fear of...", which is:

J'ai peur de...
(zhay purr duh)

So, how would you say "I'm scared of going back to Paris" (literally "I have fear of to return to Paris")?

J'ai peur de retourner à Paris.
(zhay purr duh ruh-toor-nay a pa-ree)

How about "I'm scared of going back to France"?

J'ai peur de retourner en France.
(zhay purr duh ruh-toor-nay on fronce)

And "I'm scared of going back to France in September"?

J'ai peur de retourner en France en septembre.
(zhay purr duh ruh-toor-nay on fronce on sep-tom-bruh)

To say "I'm scared of flying" in French, you will literally say "I have fear of the plane". "The plane" in French is:

l'avion
(lav-ee-on)

How would you say "I'm scared of flying" (literally "I have fear of the plane")?

J'ai peur de l'avion
(zhay purr duh lav-ee-on)

The word for "but" in French is:

mais
(may)

Right, how would you say "...but I'm scared of flying" (literally "...but I have fear of the plane")?

...mais j'ai peur de l'avion
(...may zhay purr duh lav-ee-on)

And again, how would you say "I feel like going back to Paris / I fancy going back to Paris" (literally "I have envy of to return to Paris")?

J'ai envie de retourner à Paris.
(zhay on-vee duh ruh-toor-nay a pa-ree)

Let's put those bits together and now say "I feel like going back to Paris but I'm scared of flying":

J'ai envie de retourner à Paris mais j'ai peur de l'avion.
(zhay *on-vee* duh ruh-*toor*-nay a pa-ree may zhay purr duh lav-ee-*on*)

Good. So again, how would you say "I feel like... / I fancy... / I have envy of..."?

J'ai envie de...
(zhay *on-vee* duh)

And how would you say "I'm scared of / I have fear of"?

J'ai peur de
(zhay purr duh)

And can you remember how to say "I'm planning to... / I have the intention of..."?

J'ai l'intention de...
(zhay *lon-ton*-syon duh)

"To take" in French is:

prendre
(pron-druh)

And "the Eurostar" in French is quite simply:

l'Eurostar
(luh-roe-star)

How would you say "to take the Eurostar"?

prendre l'Eurostar
(pron-druh luh-roe-star)

Next, how would you say "I'm planning to take the Eurostar"?

J'ai l'intention de prendre l'Eurostar.
(zhay *lon-ton*-syon duh pron-druh luh-roe-star)

"So" in French is:

alors
(a-law)

With this in mind, how would you say "…so I'm planning to take the Eurostar"?

…alors j'ai l'intention de prendre l'Eurostar.
(a-law zhay lon-ton-syon duh pron-druh luh-roe-star)

And again, how would you say "I'm frightened of flying"?

J'ai peur de l'avion.
(zhay purr duh lav-ee-on)

Knowing this, how would you say "I'm frightened of flying so I'm planning to take the Eurostar"?

J'ai peur de l'avion, alors j'ai l'intention de prendre l'Eurostar.
(zhay purr duh lav-ee-on, a-law zhay lon-ton-syon duh pron-druh luh-roe-star)

Alright, how would you say "I feel like… / I fancy…" in French?

J'ai envie de…
(zhay on-vee duh)

Extend this now, saying "I feel like going back to Paris":

J'ai envie de retourner à Paris.
(zhay on-vee duh ruh-toor-nay a pa-ree)

And remind me, what is "but" in French?

mais
(may)

Now, how would you say, "I feel like going back to Paris but I'm scared of flying, so I'm planning to take the Eurostar"? Take your time with this sentence, building it slowly, bit by bit, and think out each part as you work through it.

J'ai envie de retourner à Paris mais j'ai peur de l'avion, alors j'ai l'intention de prendre l'Eurostar.
(zhay on-vee duh ruh-toor-nay a pa-ree may zhay purr duh lav-ee-on, a-law zhay lon-ton-syon duh pron-druh luh-roe-star)

It's a long and complex sentence, so feel free to go through it a few times even once you get it right.

Okay, let's try putting this together with the rest of the dialogue from the beginning of the chapter. You already know almost everything you need for it.

Start by being Person 1 from the dialogue and say "I feel like going back to France in May":

J'ai envie de retourner en France en mai.
(zhay on-vee duh ruh-toor-nay on fronce on mey)

Person 2 is now going to reply to this simply by saying "really?" "Really" in French is:

vraiment
(vray-mon)

Reply to that earlier statement saying simply "really?":

vraiment ?
(vray-mon)

"Yes" in French is:

Oui
(wee)

You reply to Person 2, saying "Yes, I feel like going back to Paris but I'm scared of flying, so I'm planning to take the Eurostar." How will you say that? Again, take your time:

Oui, j'ai envie de retourner à Paris mais j'ai peur de l'avion, alors j'ai l'intention de prendre l'Eurostar.
(wee zhay on-vee duh ruh-toor-nay a pa-ree may zhay purr duh lav-ee-on, a-law zhay lon-ton-syon duh pron-druh luh-roe-star)

Good. Now, with that done, try going through the dialogue all in one go below:

I'm planning to go back to France in May:

J'ai l'intention de retourner en France en mai.
(zhay lon-ton-syon duh ruh-toor-nay on fronce on mey)

Really?
Vraiment?
(vray-mon)

Yes, I feel like going back to Paris but I'm scared of flying, so I'm planning to take the Eurostar.

Oui, j'ai envie de retourner à Paris mais j'ai peur de l'avion, alors j'ai l'intention de prendre l'Eurostar.
(wee zhay on-vee duh ruh-toor-nay a pa-ree may zhay purr duh lav-ee-on, a-law zhay lon-ton-syon duh pron-druh luh-roe-star)

That was an extremely complex dialogue which contained a lot of different ideas and phrases that needed to be juggled. If you felt unclear regarding how to construct any of the different parts it was made up of, do go back to the beginning of the chapter. And you should feel free to do this at any point when you feel that constructing a sentence is becoming a struggle. There is no rush. You should always only work at a pace that feels suitable to you. And, when you do get to the point where you can get through this entire dialogue without making any mistakes, it can still be worth practising it a few times. This will help build your fluency and confidence in using what you've learnt.

If you've done all that, then you can look forward to expanding and developing this dialogue even further as you venture into the next chapter.

It's time again to add some new building blocks. Here they are:

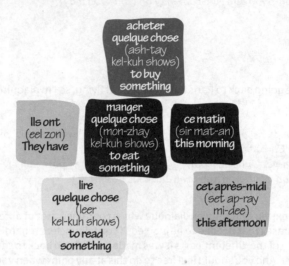

**acheter
quelque chose**
(ash-tay
kel-kuh shows)
**to buy
something**

Ils ont
(eel zon)
They have

**manger
quelque chose**
(mon-zhay
kel-kuh shows)
**to eat
something**

ce matin
(sir mat-an)
this morning

**lire
quelque chose**
(leer
kel-kuh shows)
**to read
something**

cet après-midi
(set ap-ray
mi-dee)
this afternoon

You now have your new building blocks. Make as many sentences as you can!

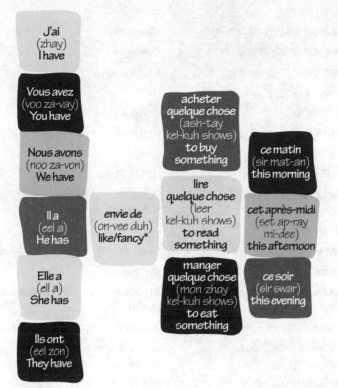

J'ai
(zhay)
I have

Vous avez
(voo za-vay)
You have

Nous avons
(noo za-von)
We have

Il a
(eel a)
He has

Elle a
(ell a)
She has

Ils ont
(eel zon)
They have

envie de
(on-vee duh)
*like/fancy**

**acheter
quelque chose**
(ash-tay
kel-kuh shows)
**to buy
something**

**lire
quelque chose**
(leer
kel-kuh shows)
**to read
something**

**manger
quelque chose**
(mon-zhay
kel-kuh shows)
**to eat
something**

ce matin
(sir mat-an)
this morning

cet après-midi
(set ap-ray
mi-dee)
this afternoon

ce soir
(sir swar)
this evening

* literally "envy of".

Checklist 3

You know what to do with the checklist now, so you don't need to be reminded about that.

Do bear one thing in mind though. The checklists don't need to be done in one sitting. So, if you get through a page or two and feel that's enough, then simply leave the rest until the next day. Always work at your own pace and don't do so much that you end up feeling overwhelmed. "Steady as she goes" should be your mantra!

le week-end (luh weekend)	the weekend
panique (pan-eek)	panic
stratégique (stra-tay-zheek)	strategic
biologique (bee-ol-oh-zheek)	biological
technologique (tek-nol-oh-zheek)	technological
J'ai (zhay)	I have
visité (visit-ay)	visited
J'ai visité (zhay visit-ay)	I have visited / I visited / I did visit
Paris (pa-ree)	Paris
Notre-Dame (not-re darm)	Notre-Dame
J'ai visité Notre-Dame. (zhay visit-ay not-re darm)	I have visited Notre-Dame / I visited Notre-Dame / I did visit Notre-Dame.
passé (pass-ay)	spent
J'ai passé (zhay pass-ay)	I have spent / I spent / I did spend
Vous avez (voo za-vay)	You have
Vous avez passé (voo za-vay pass-ay)	You have spent / You spent / You did spend
Nous avons (noo za-von)	We have
Nous avons passé (noo za-von pass-ay)	We have spent / We spent / We did spend
septembre (sep-tom-bruh)	September
Noël (no-ell)	Christmas
à Paris (a pa-ree)	in Paris
en France (on fronce)	in France
en Suisse (on swees)	in Switzerland
Nous avons passé Noël en Suisse. (noo za-von pass-ay no-ell on swees)	We have spent Christmas in Switzerland / We spent Christmas in Switzerland / We did spend Christmas in Switzerland.
Vous avez passé septembre en France. (voo za-vay pass-ay sep-tom-bruh on fronce)	You have spent September in France / You spent September in France / You did spend September in France.
et (ay)	and

c'était (set-ay)	it was
C'était fantastique. (set-ay fon-tass-teek)	It was fantastic.
très agréable (trez ag-ray-arb-luh)	lovely / very agreeable
C'était très agréable. (set-ay trez ag-ray-arb-luh)	It was lovely. / It was very agreeable.
J'ai passé le week-end à Paris… et c'était très agréable. (zhay pass-ay luh weekend a pa-ree… ay set-ay trez ag-ray-arb-luh)	I spent the weekend in Paris… and it was lovely.
situation[4] (sit-yoo-ass-yon)	situation
organisation (or-gan-ee-zass-yon)	organisation
communication (com-you-nik-ass-yon)	communication
invité (earn-vit-ay)	invited
préparé (pray-par-ay)	prepared
réservé (ray-zurv-ay)	reserved / booked
commandé (comm-on-day)	ordered
payé (pay-ay)	paid
fait (fay)	done
l'addition (la-dis-yon)	the bill
le dîner (luh din-ay)	the dinner
le rosbif (luh ros-beef)	the roast beef
une table (oon tarb-luh)	a table
une chambre (oon shom-bruh)	a room
un taxi (urn taxi)	a taxi
J'ai préparé le dîner. (zhay pray-par-ay luh din-ay)	I have prepared the dinner / I prepared the dinner / I did prepare the dinner.
J'ai commandé le rosbif pour le dîner. (zhay comm-on-day luh ros-beef poor luh din-ay)	I have ordered roast beef for dinner / I ordered roast beef for dinner / I did order roast beef for dinner.

---

4   Again, you'll notice, as I did before with the "ic" / "ical" Word Robbery, I have now also added a greater variety of "ion" words so that you get more practice with "ion" conversions.

J'ai réservé une table pour vous. (zhay ray-zurv-ay oon tarb-luh poor voo)	I have booked a table for you / I booked a table for you / I did book a table for you.
Elle a (ell a)	She has
Elle a réservé une table pour ce soir. (ell a ray-zurv-ay oon tarb-luh poor sir swar)	She has booked / reserved a table for this evening – She booked / reserved a table for this evening – She did book / reserve a table for this evening.
Il a (eel a)	He has
Il a réservé une chambre pour deux personnes. (eel a ray-zurv-ay oon shom-bruh poor duh purse-on)	He has booked / reserved a room for two people – He booked / reserved a room for two people – He did book / reserve a room for two people.
Nous avons réservé un taxi pour vous. (noo za-von ray-zur-vay urn taxi poor voo)	We have booked a taxi for you / We booked a taxi for you / We did book a taxi for you.
Nous avons payé l'addition. (noo za-von pay-ay la-dis-yon)	We paid the bill / We have paid the bill / We did pay the bill.
Qu'est-ce que ? (kess-kuh)	What? / What is it that?
Qu'est-ce que vous avez préparé ? (kess-kuh voo za-vay pray-par-ay)	What have you prepared? / What did you prepare? (literally "What is it that you have prepared?")
Qu'est-ce que vous avez fait ? (kess-kuh voo za-vay fay)	What have you done? / What did you do? (literally "What is it that you have done?")
J'ai réservé une table, commandé le dîner et puis payé l'addition. Qu'est-ce que vous avez fait ? (zhay ray-zurv-ay oon tarb-luh, comm-on-day luh din-ay ay pwee pay-ay la-dis-yon. kess-kuh voo za-vay fay)	I booked a table, ordered dinner and then paid the bill. What did you do?
J'ai l'intention de… (zhay lon-ton-syon duh)	I'm planning to… (literally "I have the intention of…")
J'ai l'intention de retourner en France en mai. (zhay lon-ton-syon duh ruh-toor-nay on fronce on mey)	I'm planning to go back to France in May.

J'ai peur de… (zhay purr duh)	I'm scared of… (literally "I have fear of…")
J'ai peur de retourner en France en septembre. (zhay purr duh ruh-toor-nay on fronce on sep-tom-bruh)	I'm scared of going back to France in September.
Vraiment ? (vray-mon)	Really?
alors (a-law)	so
mais (may)	but
J'ai envie de… (zhay on-vee duh)	I feel like… / I fancy… (literally "I have envy of…")
Oui, j'ai envie de retourner à Paris mais j'ai peur de l'avion, alors j'ai l'intention de prendre l'Eurostar. (wee zhay on-vee duh ruh-toor-nay a pa-ree may zhay purr duh lav-ee-on, a-law zhay lon-ton-syon duh pron-druh luh-roe-star)	Yes, I feel like going back to Paris but I'm scared of flying, so I'm planning to take the Eurostar.
J'ai envie d'acheter quelque chose ce matin. (zhay on-vee dash-tay kel-kuh shows sir mat-an)	I feel like / fancy buying something this morning.
Il a envie de lire quelque chose cet après-midi. (eel a on-vee duh leer kel-kuh shows set ap-ray mi-dee)	He feels like / fancies reading something this afternoon.
Ils ont (eel zon)	They have
Ils ont envie de manger quelque chose ce soir. (eel zon on-vee duh mon-zhay kel-kuh shows sir swar)	They feel like eating something this evening.

Now, time to do it the other way around!

the weekend	**le week-end** (luh weekend)
panic	**panique** (pan-eek)
strategic	**stratégique** (stra-tay-zheek)
biological	**biologique** (bee-ol-oh-zheek)
technological	**technologique** (tek-nol-oh-zheek)

I have	J'ai (zhay)
visited	visité (visit-ay)
I have visited / I visited / I did visit	J'ai visité (zhay visit-ay)
Paris	Paris (pa-ree)
Notre-Dame	Notre-Dame (not-re darm)
I have visited Notre-Dame / I visited Notre-Dame / I did visit Notre-Dame.	J'ai visité Notre-Dame. (zhay visit-ay not-re darm)
spent	passé (pass-ay)
I have spent / I spent / I did spend	J'ai passé (zhay pass-ay)
You have	Vous avez (voo za-vay)
You have spent / You spent / You did spend	Vous avez passé (voo za-vay pass-ay)
We have	Nous avons (noo za-von)
We have spent / We spent / We did spend	Nous avons passé (noo za-von pass-ay)
September	septembre (sep-tom-bruh)
Christmas	Noël (no-ell)
in Paris	à Paris (a pa-ree)
in France	en France (on fronce)
in Switzerland	en Suisse (on swees)
We have spent Christmas in Switzerland / We spent Christmas in Switzerland / We did spend Christmas in Switzerland.	Nous avons passé Noël en Suisse. (noo za-von pass-ay no-ell on swees)
You have spent September in France / You spent September in France / You did spend September in France.	Vous avez passé septembre en France. (voo za-vay pass-ay sep-tom-bruh on fronce)
and	et (ay)
it was	c'était (set-ay)
It was fantastic.	C'était fantastique. (set-ay fon-tass-teek)
lovely / very agreeable	très agréable (trez ag-ray-arb-luh)
It was lovely. / It was very agreeable.	C'était très agréable. (set-ay trez ag-ray-arb-luh)

I spent the weekend in Paris… and it was lovely.	J'ai passé le week-end à Paris… et c'était très agréable. (zhay pass-ay luh weekend a pa-ree… ay set-ay trez ag-ray-arb-luh)
situation	situation (sit-yoo-ass-yon)
organisation	organisation (or-gan-ee-zass-yon)
communication	communication (com-you-nik-ass-yon)
invited	invité (earn-vit-ay)
prepared	préparé (pray-par-ay)
reserved / booked	réservé (ray-zurv-ay)
ordered	commandé (comm-on-day)
paid	payé (pay-ay)
done	fait (fay)
the bill	l'addition (la-dis-yon)
the dinner	le dîner (luh din-ay)
the roast beef	le rosbif (luh ros-beef)
a table	une table (oon tarb-luh)
a room	une chambre (oon shom-bruh)
a taxi	un taxi (urn taxi)
I have prepared the dinner / I prepared the dinner / I did prepare the dinner.	J'ai préparé le dîner. (zhay pray-par-ay luh din-ay)
I have ordered roast beef for dinner / I ordered roast beef for dinner / I did order roast beef for dinner.	J'ai commandé le rosbif pour le dîner. (zhay comm-on-day luh ros-beef poor luh din-ay)
I have booked a table for you / I booked a table for you / I did book a table for you.	J'ai réservé une table pour vous. (zhay ray-zurv-ay oon tarb-luh poor voo)
She has	Elle a (ell a)
She has booked / reserved a table for this evening – She booked / reserved a table for this evening – She did book / reserve a table for this evening.	Elle a réservé une table pour ce soir. (ell a ray-zurv-ay oon tarb-luh poor sir swar)

He has	Il a (eel a)
He has booked / reserved a room for two people – He booked / reserved a room for two people – He did book / reserve a room for two people.	Il a réservé une chambre pour deux personnes. (eel a ray-zurv-ay oon shom-bruh poor duh purse-on)
We have booked a taxi for you / We booked a taxi for you / We did book a taxi for you.	Nous avons réservé un taxi pour vous. (noo za-von ray-zur-vay urn taxi poor voo)
We paid the bill / We have paid the bill / We did pay the bill.	Nous avons payé l'addition. (noo za-von pay-ay la-dis-yon)
What? / What is it that?	Qu'est-ce que ? (kess-kuh)
What have you prepared? / What did you prepare?	Qu'est-ce que vous avez préparé ? (kess-kuh voo za-vay pray-par-ay)
What have you done? / What did you do?	Qu'est-ce que vous avez fait ? (kess-kuh voo za-vay fay)
I booked a table, ordered dinner and then paid the bill. What did you do?	J'ai réservé une table, commandé le dîner et puis payé l'addition. Qu'est-ce que vous avez fait ? (zhay ray-zurv-ay oon tarb-luh, comm-on-day luh din-ay ay pwee pay-ay la-dis-yon. kess-kuh voo za-vay fay)
I'm planning to… (literally "I have the intention of…")	J'ai l'intention de… (zhay lon-ton-syon duh)
I'm planning to go back to France in May.	J'ai l'intention de retourner en France en mai. (zhay lon-ton-syon duh ruh-toor-nay on fronce on mey)
I'm scared of… (literally "I have fear of…")	J'ai peur de… (zhay purr duh)
I'm scared of going back to France in September.	J'ai peur de retourner en France en septembre. (zhay purr duh ruh-toor-nay on fronce on sep-tom-bruh)
Really?	Vraiment ? (vray-mon)
so	alors (a-law)
but	mais (may)
I feel like… / I fancy… (literally "I have envy of…")	J'ai envie de… (zhay on-vee duh)

Yes, I feel like going back to Paris but I'm scared of flying, so I'm planning to take the Eurostar.	Oui, j'ai envie de retourner à Paris mais j'ai peur de l'avion, alors j'ai l'intention de prendre l'Eurostar. (wee zhay on-vee duh ruh-toor-nay a pa-ree may zhay purr duh lav-ee-on, a-law zhay lon-ton-syon duh pron-druh luh-roe-star)
I feel like / fancy buying something this morning.	J'ai envie d'acheter quelque chose ce matin. (zhay on-vee dash-tay kel-kuh shows sir mat-an)
He feels like / fancies reading something this afternoon.	Il a envie de lire quelque chose cet après-midi. (eel a on-vee duh leer kel-kuh shows set ap-ray mi-dee)
They have	Ils ont (eel zon)
They feel like eating something this evening.	Ils ont envie de manger quelque chose ce soir. (eel zon on-vee duh mon-zhay kel-kuh shows sir swar)

Well, that's it, you're done with Chapter 3. Take a break!

How to learn the French days of the week in an easy and meaningful way!

Do you know the days of the week in French?

Well, whether you do or don't, most people aren't aware what the days of the week actually mean in French. If they were, they might be surprised how much easier to remember, more meaningful and more beautiful they become.

Let's take a look at them!

Monday – lundi

Monday, in English, actually means "Moon's Day" and the same is true in French. The French use their word for moon, which is "lune" (think "lunar") and then add the Latin word for "day" to the end it, making "lundi" – Moonday / Monday.

Tuesday – mardi

If Monday in French is dedicated to the moon, Tuesday is dedicated to Mars. To make Tuesday in French we take the word "Mars", remove the "s" from the end, and again add the Latin word for "day" to the end of it, making "mardi" – Mars's Day / Tuesday.

Wednesday – mercredi

Ah, here we are now at Wednesday or "Woden's Day" as it really should read in English. Whereas in English Wednesday celebrates the god Woden, in French it celebrates Mercury. Adding the Latin word for "day" to the end makes "mercredi" – Mercury's Day / Wednesday.

Thursday – jeudi

In English, the day after Woden's Day is of course "Thor's Day", now written Thursday. In France, by contrast, the day belongs to Jove, king of the gods. So, with the Latin word for "day" on the end again, it makes "jeudi" – Jove's Day / Thursday.

Friday – vendredi

Friday in English means "Frigga's Day". "Who is Frigga?" you may ask. Well, she was Odin's wife and Thor's mother. She was also, for the earliest English people, the goddess of love. Curiously, French also names Friday after a goddess of love, Venus. So, Friday in French becomes Venus's Day – "vendredi".

Saturday – samedi

Saturday in English is "Saturn's Day". The French for Saturday, however, comes from the Latin term "sambati diēs", which means Sabbath Day, as the Sabbath was originally observed on Saturday rather than Sunday. This, in modern French, has become "samedi".

Sunday – dimanche

I'm sure you can guess the meaning of Sunday in English; clearly it is the Sun's Day. In French though, its sound comes from Latin again – from "diēs Dominica" – meaning "the day of the Lord". In modern French this has simply become "dimanche".

So, there you have the days of the week in French. Hopefully they hold a little more meaning for you than they did before. If you don't know them already, you'll find them on a quick reference list on the next page. Just take a look at it each time you finish a chapter, covering up the French and seeing if you can recall it, and you'll soon pick them up.

(By the way, have you noticed that, unlike in English, days of the week in French don't need to be written with a capital letter?)

Monday	**Moon Day**	lundi	
Tuesday	**Mars Day**	mardi	
Wednesday	**Mercury Day**	mercredi	
Thursday	**Jove Day**	jeudi	
Friday	**Venus Day**	vendredi	
Saturday	**Sabbath Day**	samedi	
Sunday	**Day of the Lord**	dimanche	

CHAPTER 4

You need help, mate!

Person 1:	I'm planning to go back to France in May.
Person 2:	Really?
Person 1:	Yes, I feel like going back to Paris but I'm scared of flying, so I'm planning to take the Eurostar.
Person 2:	Really? You're scared of flying?
Person 1:	Yes, I can't stand planes!
Person 2:	You need help, mate!

As you can see, I have extended the dialogue from the previous chapter. You are now going to learn how to complete this conversation by building on what you've learnt already. You will also expand your range of everyday French expressions as you go.

So, remind me now, how would you say "I'm planning to..."?

J'ai l'intention de...
(zhay lon-ton-syon duh)

And how would you say "I'm planning to go back to France in May"?

J'ai l'intention de retourner en France en mai.
(zhay lon-ton-syon duh ruh-toor-nay on fronce on mey)

How would someone reply to that, saying "really?"

Vraiment ?
(vray-mon)

And again, what was "I feel like..." in French?

J'ai envie de...
(zhay on-vee duh)

So, how would you say "I feel like going back to France / I fancy going back to France"?

J'ai envie de retourner en France.
(zhay on-vee duh ruh-toor-nay on fronce)

How about "I feel like going back to Paris / I fancy going back to Paris"?

J'ai envie de retourner à Paris.
(zhay on-vee duh ruh-toor-nay a pa-ree)

And how would you say "I'm scared of…" in French?

J'ai peur de…
(zhay purr duh)

What about "I'm scared of flying"?

J'ai peur de l'avion.
(zhay purr duh lav-ee-on)

Finally, just as at the end of the previous chapter, give an answer saying "Yes, I feel like going back to Paris but I'm scared of flying, so I'm planning to take the Eurostar."

Oui, j'ai envie de retourner à Paris mais j'ai peur de l'avion, alors j'ai l'intention de prendre l'Eurostar.
(wee zhay on-vee duh ruh-toor-nay a pa-ree may zhay purr duh lav-ee-on, a-law zhay lon-ton-syon duh pron-druh luh-roe-star)

In the first part of the dialogue you learnt "I'm planning to..." (literally "I have the intention of..."), which was:

J'ai l'intention de...
(zhay lon-ton-syon duh)

You also learnt "I feel like... / I fancy..." (literally "I have envy of..."), which was:

J'ai envie de...
(zhay on-vee duh)

And finally you learnt "I'm scared of..." (literally "I have fear of..."), which was:

J'ai peur de...
(zhay purr duh)

These are all useful phrases that are constructed in a similar way. I'm going to introduce you to just two more similarly structured phrases, so that you can complete the dialogue. As you're familiar with how these types of phrases work already, you should find using them pretty easy.

To say "I can't stand..." in French, you will literally say "I have horror of...", which in French is:

J'ai horreur de...
(zhay o-rurr-duh)

So, to say "I can't stand flying!", for instance, you will literally say "I have horror of the plane!" How do you think you would say that?

J'ai horreur de l'avion !
(zhay o-rurr-duh lav-ee-on)

What was the word for "Christmas" in French?

Noël
(no-ell)

So, how would you say "I can't stand Christmas!"?

J'ai horreur de Noël !
(zhay o-rurr-duh no-ell)

Again, what is "we have"?

Nous avons
(noo za-von)

How would you say "we can't stand Christmas!" (literally "we have horror of Christmas")?

Nous avons horreur de Noël !
(noo za-von o-rurr-duh no-ell)

How about "we can't stand flying!"?

Nous avons horreur de l'avion !
(noo za-von o-rurr-duh lav-ee-on)

What is "he has"?

Il a
(eel a)

And so how would you say "he can't stand flying!"?

Il a horreur de l'avion !
(eel a o-rurr-duh lav-ee-on)

What is "she has"?

Elle a
(ell a)

So how would you say "she can't stand flying!"?

Elle a horreur de l'avion !
(ell a o-rurr-duh lav-ee-on)

What is "they have"?

Ils ont
(eel zon)

And "they can't stand flying!"?

Ils ont horreur de l'avion !
(eel zon o-rurr-duh lav-ee-on)

Finally, what is "you have"?

Vous avez
(voo za-vay)

So how would you say "you can't stand flying!"?

Vous avez horreur de l'avion !
(voo za-vay o-rurr-duh lav-ee-on)

You can very easily turn this statement – "you can't stand flying!" – into a question in French. All you need to do is raise your voice at the end of the sentence. By doing this, you will ask "you can't stand flying?" – literally "you have horror of the plane?". Do that now:

Vous avez horreur de l'avion ?
(voo za-vay o-rurr-duh lav-ee-on)

Now try "you can't stand Christmas?" (literally "you have horror of Christmas?"):

Vous avez horreur de Noël ?
(voo za-vay o-rurr-duh no-ell)

How to say "you" in French

So far, you have been using "vous avez" to mean "you have" in French. The "avez" is the bit that means "have" and the "vous" is the bit that means "you".

However, "vous" is not the only word in French that means "you". In fact, it is the formal word for "you". So, if you're meeting another person for the first time, or if you're talking to someone you do not know very well, you will use "vous" when addressing them.

However, if you make a close friend, or if you have family in France, you will not use "vous" when you talk to one of them. Instead, you will use the informal, familiar word for "you", which is "tu".

Let's start using this below.

"You have" (informal) in French is:

Tu as
(tü[5] a)

So how would you say "you can't stand Christmas" (informal)?

Tu as horreur de Noël
(Tü a o-rurr-duh no-ell)

And how would you say "you can't stand flying" (informal)?

Tu as horreur de l'avion
(Tü a o-rurr-duh lav-ee-on)

---

5   Oh dear, what on earth is this "ü"? Well, it is used here to represent a sound that doesn't actually exist in English. Fear not though, as I'm going to show you how you can make this sound without any difficulty. To make this unfamiliar "ü" sound, the first thing you need to do is to round your lips as though you are going to whistle but then, instead of whistling, keep your lips perfectly round and say the letter "e". This will give you the mysterious "ü" sound that you need to pronounce "tu" correctly. So again, whilst keeping your lips in a rounded shape (like you would for whistling) say the letter "e". You now have the "ü" sound, so now use it to make the word "tu" (tü) – it may take a bit of practice!

How about, "you're scared of flying" (informal) (literally "you have fear of the plane")?

Tu *as peur de* l'avion.
(Tü a purr-duh lav-ee-on)

Turn this into a question now by raising your voice at the end of the sentence. Ask "you're scared of flying?" (informal):

Tu *as peur de* l'avion ?
(Tü a purr-duh lav-ee-on)

And again, how would you say "I'm scared of flying"?

J'ai *peur de* l'avion.
(zhay purr-duh lav-ee-on)

And "I can't stand flying!" (literally "I have horror of the plane")?

J'ai *horreur de* l'avion !
(zhay o-rurr-duh lav-ee-on)

Let's assume someone has just asked you if you're scared of flying and you want to answer, "yes, I can't stand flying!":

Oui, j'ai *horreur de* l'avion !
(wee zhay o-rurr-duh lav-ee-on)

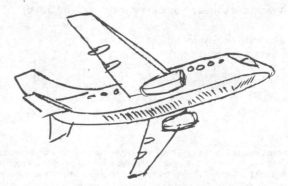

Alright, if you have reached this point, then you have had plenty of practice saying "I'm planning to…", "I feel like…", "I can't stand…" and "I'm frightened of…".

Now, as I've said before, please don't try to memorise these phrases or even make any effort to remember them. All you need to do is work your way through this book and follow its instructions. Everything introduced will come up again, multiple times. Sometimes you will forget things as I introduce new words and constructions but this is all part of the method that I am using to teach you.

So, let's introduce the final phrase from this group of similarly constructed expressions and head on towards the end of the chapter.

This time you're going to learn how to say "I need…", which in French is said literally as "I have need of…" This is:

J'ai besoin de…
(zhay burz-won duh)

So, how would you say "I need a taxi"?

J'ai besoin d'un taxi.
(zhay burz-won durn taxi)

You'll notice that when you have "de" next to "un" the two words shorten to "d'un". This is nothing to worry about. It just makes the two words easier to pronounce together. If you said "de un" instead of shortening it as you're supposed to, you would still be understood but, as you get more practice speaking the language, you will simply find that you naturally begin to contract "de un" into "d'un" as it just becomes easier to do so than to say them separately.

Now again, what is "a room" in French?

une chambre
(oon shom-bruh)

So how would you say "I need a room"?

J'ai besoin d'une chambre.
(zhay burz-won doon shom-bruh)

Again, you notice that just as "de un" is shortened to "d'un", so also is "de une" shortened to "d'une".

In fact, when "de" is followed by a word beginning with a vowel (a,e,i,o,u) it tends to contract. As I've already mentioned though, this isn't something to worry about, as you'll simply find yourself doing this instinctively after a while because it's just easier to pronounce it that way.

"To speak" or "to talk" in French is:

parler
(par-lay)

How would you say "I need to speak" (literally "I have need of to speak")?

J'ai besoin de parler.
(zhay burz-won duh par-lay)

"French" in French is:

français
(fron-say)

How would you say "I need to speak French"?

J'ai besoin de parler français.
(zhay burz-won duh par-lay fron-say)

Now, what is "you have" (formal)?

Vous avez
(voo za-vay)

And what is "you have" (informal)?

Tu as
(tü a)

So how would you say "you need to speak French" (informal) – (literally "you have need of to speak French")?

Tu as besoin de parler français.
(tü a burz-won duh par-lay fron-say)

How about "you need a room" (informal) – (literally "you have need of a room")?

Tu as besoin d'une chambre.
(tü a burz-won doon shom-bruh)

What about "you need a taxi" (informal)?

Tu as besoin d'un taxi.
(tü a burz-won durn taxi)

"Help" in French is literally "aid", which in French is spelt:

aide
(aid)

So, how would you say "you need help" (informal)?

Tu as besoin d'aide.
(tü a burz-won daid)

The word for "mate", "pal", "buddy" and so on, in French is "pote" and French speakers like to refer to such a person as "my mate", "my pal" and so on, which in French is:

mon pote
(mon pote)

Okay, how would you say "you need help, mate!"?

Tu as besoin d'aide, mon pote !
(tü a burz-won daid, mon pote)

Alright, let's review some of these phrases again.
First of all, how would you say "I'm planning to…"?

J'ai l'intention de…
(zhay lon-ton-syon duh)

And how would you say "I feel like… / I fancy…"?

J'ai envie de…
(zhay on-vee duh)

How about "I'm scared of..."?

J'ai peur de...
(zhay purr-duh)

And "I can't stand..."?

J'ai horreur de...
(zhay o-rurr-duh)

And finally "I need..."?

J'ai besoin de...
(zhay burz-won duh)

So, how would you say "I need to speak French"?

J'ai besoin de parler français.
(zhay burz-won duh par-lay fron-say)

What about "I feel like speaking French"?

J'ai envie de parler français.
(zhay on-vee duh par-lay fron-say)

And "I'm scared of speaking French"?

J'ai peur de parler français.
(zhay purr-duh par-lay fron-say)

"I'm planning to speak French"?

J'ai l'intention de parler français.
(zhay lon-ton-syon duh par-lay fron-say)

And how would you say "I'm planning to go back to France in May"?

J'ai l'intention de retourner en France en mai.
(zhay lon-ton-syon duh ruh-toor-nay on fronce on mey)

How about "I'm scared of going back to France in May"?

J'ai peur de retourner en France en mai.
(zhay purr-duh ruh-toor-nay on fronce on mey)

"I feel like going back to France in May"?

J'ai envie de retourner en France en mai.
(zhay on-vee duh ruh-toor-nay on fronce on mey)

"I need to go back to France in May"?

J'ai besoin de retourner en France en mai.
(zhay burz-won duh ruh-toor-nay on fronce on mey)

You are probably starting to get a feel now for just how useful – and interchangeable – these phrases are, depending on what exactly it is you want to say.

Now again, how would you say "I can't stand flying!"?

J'ai horreur de l'avion !
(zhay o-rurr-duh lav-ee-on)

And how would you say "I can't stand Christmas!"?

J'ai horreur de Noël !
(zhay o-rurr-duh no-ell)

What is "to take"?

prendre
pron-druh

And how about "to take the Eurostar"?

prendre l'Eurostar
(pron-druh luh-roe-star)

So how would you say "I can't stand taking the Eurostar"?

J'ai horreur de prendre l'Eurostar.
(zhay o-rurr-duh pron-druh luh-roe-star)

How would someone you said that to ask you "really?"?

Vraiment ?
(vray-mon)

And how would you say "I'm planning to take the Eurostar"?

J'ai l'intention de prendre l'Eurostar.
(zhay lon-ton-syon duh pron-druh luh-roe-star)

How about "I feel like going back to Paris"?

J'ai envie de retourner à Paris.
(zhay on-vee duh ruh-toor-nay a pa-ree)

And what about "I'm scared of flying"?

J'ai peur de l'avion.
(zhay purr-duh lav-ee-on)

What is the word for "but" in French?

mais
(may)

And what is the word for "so"?

alors
(a-law)

So how would you say "I feel like going back to Paris but I'm scared of flying,
so I'm planning to take the Eurostar"?

J'ai envie de retourner à Paris mais j'ai peur de l'avion, alors j'ai l'intention
de prendre l'Eurostar.
(zhay on-vee duh ruh-toor-nay a pa-ree may zhay purr duh lav-ee-on a-law
zhay lon-ton-syon duh pron-druh luh-roe-star)

What is "you have" (informal)?

Tu as
(tü a)

So how would you say informally "you feel like going back to Paris" (literally "you have envy of to return to Paris")?

Tu as envie de retourner à Paris.
(tü a on-vee duh ruh-toor-nay a pa-ree)

How about "you are scared of flying" (informal)?

Tu as peur de l'avion.
(Tü a purr-duh lav-ee-on)

Turn this into a question by raising your voice at the end and ask "you are scared of flying?" (informal):

Tu as peur de l'avion ?
(Tü a purr-duh lav-ee-on)

How would someone answer "Yes, I can't stand flying"?

Oui, j'ai horreur de l'avion.
(wee zhay o-rurr-duh lav-ee-on)

And again, how would you say "I need…" (literally "I have need of…")?

J'ai besoin de…
(zhay burz-won duh)

And how would you say "I need help" (literally "I have need of aid")?

J'ai besoin d'aide.
(zhay burz-won daid)

And how would you say informally "You need help" (literally "you have need of aid")?

Tu as besoin d'aide.
(tü a burz-won daid)

And how would you say "mate" (literally "my mate" in French)?

mon pote
(mon pote)

Put this together now and say "You need help, mate!" (informal):

Tu as besoin d'aide, mon pote !
(tü a burz-won daid, mon pote)

Okay, you're ready now to make an attempt at doing the entire dialogue by yourself. Take each sentence slowly and, if you get it wrong, just take another stab at it. It isn't a race and you should just take your time to work it out.

Have a go now:

Person 1:	I'm planning to go back to France in May.
	J'ai l'intention de retourner en France en mai.
	(zhay lon-ton-syon duh ruh-toor-nay on fronce on mey)

Person 2:	Really?
	Vraiment ?
	(vray-mon)

Person 1:	Yes, I feel like going back to Paris but I'm scared of flying, so I'm planning to take the Eurostar.
	Oui, j'ai envie de retourner à Paris mais j'ai peur de l'avion, alors j'ai l'intention de prendre l'Eurostar.
	(wee zhay on-vee duh ruh-toor-nay a pa-ree may zhay purr duh lav-ee-on, a-law zhay lon-ton-syon duh pron-druh luh-roe-star)

Person 2:	Really? You're scared of flying?
	Vraiment ? Tu as peur de l'avion ?
	(vray-mon tü a purr-duh lav-ee-on)

Person 1:	Yes, I can't stand planes!
	Oui, j'ai horreur de l'avion !
	(wee zhay o-rurr-duh lav-ee-on)

Person 2:	You need help, mate!
	Tu as besoin d'aide, mon pote !
	(tü a burz-won daid, mon pote)

How did that go? It's fairly complex stuff but as you're probably beginning to notice it is also just a matter of patterns. Learn the patterns and you'll find you can very quickly begin to communicate in the language – and with a minimum of effort!

Building Blocks 4

Okay. Building block time. Here they are:

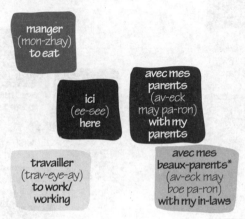

manger
(mon-zhay)
to eat

ici
(ee-see)
here

avec mes parents
(av-eck may pa-ron)
with my parents

travailler
(trav-eye-ay)
to work/working

avec mes beaux-parents*
(av-eck may boe pa-ron)
with my in-laws

* the term for in-laws in French literally means "beautiful parents" – yes, try not to laugh!

As before, use the building blocks below to make as many sentences as you can. Make sure to use every word at least once or, preferably, several times.

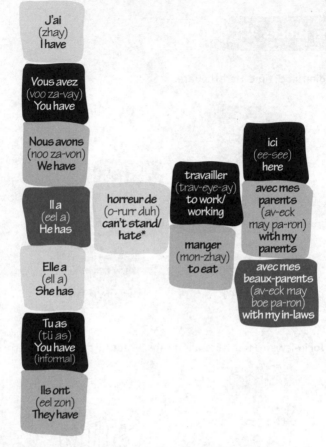

J'ai
(zhay)
I have

Vous avez
(voo za-vay)
You have

Nous avons
(noo za-von)
We have

Il a
(eel a)
He has

Elle a
(ell a)
She has

Tu as
(tü as)
You have (informal)

Ils ont
(eel zon)
They have

horreur de
(o-rurr duh)
can't stand/ hate*

travailler
(trav-eye-ay)
to work/ working

manger
(mon-zhay)
to eat

ici
(ee-see)
here

avec mes parents
(av-eck may pa-ron)
with my parents

avec mes beaux-parents
(av-eck may boe pa-ron)
with my in-laws

* literally "have horror of"

well, off you go then!

le week-end (luh weekend)	the weekend
électronique (ay-lek-tron-eek)	electronic
automatique (oh-toe-ma-teek)	automatic
écologique (ay-kol-oh-zheek)	ecological
chronologique (kron-ol-oh-zheek)	chronological
J'ai (zhay)	I have
visité (visit-ay)	visited
J'ai visité (zhay visit-ay)	I have visited / I visited / I did visit
Paris (pa-ree)	Paris
Notre-Dame (not-re darm)	Notre-Dame
J'ai visité Notre-Dame. (zhay visit-ay not-re darm)	I have visited Notre-Dame / I visited Notre-Dame / I did visit Notre-Dame.
passé (pass-ay)	spent
J'ai passé (zhay pass-ay)	I have spent / I spent / I did spend
Vous avez (voo za-vay)	You have
Vous avez passé (voo za-vay pass-ay)	You have spent / You spent / You did spend
Nous avons (noo za-von)	We have
Nous avons passé (noo za-von pass-ay)	We have spent / We spent / We did spend
septembre (sep-tom-bruh)	September
Noël (no-ell)	Christmas
à Paris (a pa-ree)	in Paris
en France (on fronce)	in France
en Suisse (on swees)	in Switzerland
Nous avons passé Noël en Suisse. (noo za-von pass-ay no-ell on swees)	We have spent Christmas in Switzerland / We spent Christmas in Switzerland / We did spend Christmas in Switzerland.

Vous avez passé septembre en France. (voo za-vay pass-ay sep-tom-bruh on fronce)	You have spent September in France / You spent September in France / You did spend September in France.
et (ay)	and
c'était (set-ay)	it was
C'était fantastique. (set-ay fon-tass-teek)	It was fantastic.
très agréable (trez ag-ray-arb-luh)	lovely / very agreeable
C'était très agréable. (set-ay trez ag-ray-arb-luh)	It was lovely. / It was very agreeable.
J'ai passé le week-end à Paris… et c'était très agréable. (zhay pass-ay luh weekend a pa-ree… ay set-ay trez ag-ray-arb-luh)	I spent the weekend in Paris… and it was lovely.
concentration (kon-son-trass-yon)	concentration
considération (kon-sid-air-ass-yon)	consideration
création (cray-ass-yon)	creation
invité (earn-vit-ay)	invited
préparé (pray-par-ay)	prepared
réservé (ray-zurv-ay)	reserved / booked
commandé (comm-on-day)	ordered
payé (pay-ay)	paid
fait (fay)	done
l'addition (la-dis-yon)	the bill
le dîner (luh din-ay)	the dinner
le rosbif (luh ros-beef)	the roast beef
une table (oon tarb-luh)	a table
une chambre (oon shom-bruh)	a room
un taxi (urn taxi)	a taxi
J'ai préparé le dîner. (zhay pray-par-ay luh din-ay)	I have prepared the dinner / I prepared the dinner / I did prepare the dinner.

J'ai commandé le rosbif pour le dîner. (zhay comm-on-day luh ros-beef poor luh din-ay)	I have ordered roast beef for dinner / I ordered roast beef for dinner / I did order roast beef for dinner.
J'ai réservé une table pour vous. (zhay ray-zurv-ay oon tarb-luh poor voo)	I have booked a table for you / I booked a table for you / I did book a table for you.
Elle a (ell a)	She has
Elle a réservé une table pour ce soir. (ell a ray-zurv-ay oon tarb-luh poor sir swar)	She has booked / reserved a table for this evening – She booked / reserved a table for this evening – She did book / reserve a table for this evening.
Il a (eel a)	He has
Il a réservé une chambre pour deux personnes. (eel a ray-zurv-ay oon shom-bruh poor duh purse-on)	He has booked / reserved a room for two people – He booked / reserved a room for two people – He did book / reserve a room for two people.
Nous avons réservé un taxi pour vous. (noo za-von ray-zur-vay urn taxi poor voo)	We have booked a taxi for you / We booked a taxi for you / We did book a taxi for you.
Nous avons payé l'addition. (noo za-von pay-ay la-dis-yon)	We paid the bill / We have paid the the bill / We did pay the bill.
Qu'est-ce que ? (kess-kuh)	What? / What is it that?
Qu'est-ce que vous avez préparé ? (kess-kuh voo za-vay pray-par-ay)	What have you prepared? / What did you prepare? (literally "What is it that you have prepared?")
Qu'est-ce que vous avez fait ? (kess-kuh voo za-vay fay)	What have you done? / What did you do? (literally "What is it that you have done?")
J'ai réservé une table, commandé le dîner et puis payé l'addition. Qu'est-ce que vous avez fait ? (zhay ray-zurv-ay oon tarb-luh, comm-on-day luh din-ay ay pwee pay-ay la-dis-yon. kess-kuh voo za-vay fay)	I booked a table, ordered dinner and then paid the bill. What did you do?
J'ai l'intention de… (zhay lon-ton-syon duh)	I'm planning to… / (literally "I have the intention of…")

J'ai l'intention de retourner en France en mai. (zhay lon-ton-syon duh ruh-toor-nay on fronce on mey)	I'm planning to go back to France in May.
J'ai peur de… (zhay purr duh)	I'm scared of… / (literally "I have fear of…")
J'ai peur de retourner en France en septembre. (zhay purr duh ruh-toor-nay on fronce on sep-tom-bruh)	I'm scared of going back to France in September.
Vraiment ? (vray-mon)	Really?
alors (a-law)	so
mais (may)	but
J'ai envie de… (zhay on-vee duh)	I feel like… / I fancy… / (literally "I have envy of…")
Oui, j'ai envie de retourner à Paris mais j'ai peur de l'avion, alors j'ai l'intention de prendre l'Eurostar. (wee zhay on-vee duh ruh-toor-nay a pa-ree may zhay purr duh lav-ee-on, a-law zhay lon-ton-syon duh pron-druh luh-roe-star)	Yes, I feel like going back to Paris but I'm scared of flying, so I'm planning to take the Eurostar.
J'ai envie d'acheter quelque chose ce matin. (zhay on-vee dash-tay kel-kuh shows sir mat-an)	I feel like / fancy buying something this morning.
Il a envie de lire quelque chose cet après-midi. (eel a on-vee duh leer kel-kuh shows set ap-ray mi-dee)	He feels like / fancies reading something this afternoon.
Ils ont (eel zon)	They have
Ils ont envie de manger quelque chose ce soir. (eel zon on-vee duh mon-zhay kel-kuh shows sir swar)	They feel like eating something this evening.
J'ai besoin de… (zhay burz-won duh)	I need… / (literally "I have need of…")
J'ai besoin de parler français. (zhay burz-won duh par-lay fron-say)	I need to speak French.
J'ai besoin d'un taxi. (zhay burz-won durn taxi)	I need a taxi.

J'ai besoin d'une chambre. (zhay burz-won doon shom-bruh)	I need a room.
J'ai besoin d'aide. (zhay burz-won daid)	I need help.
Tu as besoin d'aide, mon pote ! (tü a burz-won daid mon pote)	You need help, mate!
J'ai horreur de… (zhay o-rurr duh)	I can't stand… / I hate… (literally "I have horror of…")
J'ai horreur de l'avion ! (zhay o-rurr duh lav-ee-on)	I can't stand flying! / I can't stand planes! / I hate flying!
J'ai horreur de manger avec mes beaux-parents. (zhay o-rurr duh mon-zhay av-eck may boe pa-ron)	I can't stand eating with my in-laws / I hate eating with my in-laws.
Nous avons horreur de manger avec mes parents. (noo za-von o-rurr duh mon-zhay av-eck may pa-ron)	We can't stand eating with my parents / We hate eating with my parents.
Elle a horreur de travailler ici. (ell a o-rurr duh trav-eye-ay ee-see)	She can't stand working here / she hates working here.

Now, time to do it the other way around!

the weekend	**le week-end** (luh weekend)
electronic	**électronique** (ay-lek-tron-eek)
automatic	**automatique** (oh-toe-ma-teek)
ecological	**écologique** (ay-kol-oh-zheek)
chronological	**chronologique** (kron-ol-oh-zheek)
I have	**J'ai** (zhay)
visited	**visité** (visit-ay)
I have visited / I visited / I did visit	**J'ai visité** (zhay visit-ay)
Paris	**Paris** (pa-ree)
Notre-Dame	**Notre-Dame** (not-re darm)
I have visited Notre-Dame / I visited Notre-Dame / I did visit Notre-Dame.	**J'ai visité Notre-Dame.** (zhay visit-ay not-re darm)
spent	**passé** (pass-ay)

I have spent / I spent / I did spend	J'ai passé (zhay pass-ay)
You have	Vous avez (voo za-vay)
You have spent / You spent / You did spend	Vous avez passé (voo za-vay pass-ay)
We have	Nous avons (noo za-von)
We have spent / We spent / We did spend	Nous avons passé (noo za-von pass-ay)
September	septembre (sep-tom-bruh)
Christmas	Noël (no-ell)
in Paris	à Paris (a pa-ree)
in France	en France (on fronce)
in Switzerland	en Suisse (on swees)
We have spent Christmas in Switzerland / We spent Christmas in Switzerland / We did spend Christmas in Switzerland.	Nous avons passé Noël en Suisse. (noo za-von pass-ay no-ell on swees)
You have spent September in France / You spent September in France / You did spend September in France.	Vous avez passé septembre en France. (voo za-vay pass-ay sep-tom-bruh on fronce)
and	et (ay)
it was	c'était (set-ay)
It was fantastic.	C'était fantastique. (set-ay fon-tass-teek)
lovely / very agreeable	très agréable (trez ag-ray-arb-luh)
It was lovely. / It was very agreeable.	C'était très agréable. (set-ay trez ag-ray-arb-luh)
I spent the weekend in Paris… and it was lovely.	J'ai passé le week-end à Paris… et c'était très agréable. (zhay pass-ay luh weekend a pa-ree… ay set-ay trez ag-ray-arb-luh)
concentration	concentration (kon-son-trass-yon)
consideration	considération (kon-sid-air-ass-yon)
creation	création (cray-ass-yon)
invited	invité (earn-vit-ay)

prepared	**préparé** (pray-par-ay)
reserved / booked	**réservé** (ray-zurv-ay)
ordered	**commandé** (comm-on-day)
paid	**payé** (pay-ay)
done	**fait** (fay)
the bill	**l'addition** (la-dis-yon)
the dinner	**le dîner** (luh din-ay)
the roast beef	**le rosbif** (luh ros-beef)
a table	**une table** (oon tarb-luh)
a room	**une chambre** (oon shom-bruh)
a taxi	**un taxi** (urn taxi)
I have prepared the dinner / I prepared the dinner / I did prepare the dinner.	**J'ai préparé le dîner.** (zhay pray-par-ay luh din-ay)
I have ordered roast beef for dinner / I ordered roast beef for dinner / I did order roast beef for dinner.	**J'ai commandé le rosbif pour le dîner.** (zhay comm-on-day luh ros-beef poor luh din-ay)
I have booked a table for you / I booked a table for you / I did book a table for you.	**J'ai réservé une table pour vous.** (zhay ray-zurv-ay oon tarb-luh poor voo)
She has	**Elle a** (ell a)
She has booked / reserved a table for this evening – She booked / reserved a table for this evening – She did book / reserve a table for this evening.	**Elle a réservé une table pour ce soir.** (ell a ray-zurv-ay oon tarb-luh poor sir swar)
He has	**Il a** (eel a)
He has booked / reserved a room for two people – He booked / reserved a room for two people – He did book / reserve a room for two people.	**Il a réservé une chambre pour deux personnes.** (eel a ray-zurv-ay oon shom-bruh poor duh purse-on)
We have booked a taxi for you / We booked a taxi for you / We did book a taxi for you.	**Nous avons réservé un taxi pour vous.** (noo za-von ray-zur-vay urn taxi poor voo)
We paid the bill / We have paid the the bill / We did pay the bill.	**Nous avons payé l'addition.** (noo za-von pay-ay la-dis-yon)

What? / What is it that?	Qu'est-ce que ? (kess-kuh)
What have you prepared? / What did you prepare?	Qu'est-ce que vous avez préparé ? (kess-kuh voo za-vay pray-par-ay)
What have you done? / What did you do?	Qu'est-ce que vous avez fait ? (kess-kuh voo za-vay fay)
I booked a table, ordered dinner and then paid the bill. What did you do?	J'ai réservé une table, commandé le dîner et puis payé l'addition. Qu'est-ce que vous avez fait ? (zhay ray-zurv-ay oon tarb-luh, comm-on-day luh din-ay ay pwee pay-ay la-dis-yon. kess-kuh voo za-vay fay)
I'm planning to…	J'ai l'intention de… (zhay lon-ton-syon duh)
I'm planning to go back to France in May.	J'ai l'intention de retourner en France en mai. (zhay lon-ton-syon duh ruh-toor-nay on fronce on mey)
I'm scared of…	J'ai peur de… (zhay purr duh)
I'm scared of going back to France in September.	J'ai peur de retourner en France en septembre. (zhay purr duh ruh-toor-nay on fronce on sep-tom-bruh)
Really?	Vraiment ? (vray-mon)
so	alors (a-law)
but	mais (may)
I feel like… / I fancy…	J'ai envie de… (zhay on-vee duh)
Yes, I feel like going back to Paris but I'm scared of flying, so I'm planning to take the Eurostar.	Oui, j'ai envie de retourner à Paris mais j'ai peur de l'avion, alors j'ai l'intention de prendre l'Eurostar. (wee zhay on-vee duh ruh-toor-nay a pa-ree may zhay purr duh lav-ee-on, a-law zhay lon-ton-syon duh pron-druh luh-roe-star)
I feel like / fancy buying something this morning.	J'ai envie d'acheter quelque chose ce matin. (zhay on-vee dash-tay kel-kuh shows sir mat-an)
He feels like / fancies reading something this afternoon.	Il a envie de lire quelque chose cet après-midi. (eel a on-vee duh leer kel-kuh shows set ap-ray mi-dee)

They have	Ils ont (eel zon)
They feel like eating something this evening.	Ils ont envie de manger quelque chose ce soir. (eel zon on-vee duh mon-zhay kel-kuh shows sir swar)
I need… / (literally "I have need of…")	J'ai besoin de… (zhay burz-won duh)
I need to speak French.	J'ai besoin de parler français. (zhay burz-won duh par-lay fron-say)
I need a taxi.	J'ai besoin d'un taxi. (zhay burz-won durn taxi)
I need a room.	J'ai besoin d'une chambre. (zhay burz-won doon shom-bruh)
I need help.	J'ai besoin d'aide. (zhay burz-won daid)
You need help, mate!	Tu as besoin d'aide, mon pote ! (tü a burz-won daid mon pote)
I can't stand… / I hate… (literally "I have horror of…")	J'ai horreur de… (zhay o-rurr duh)
I can't stand flying! / I can't stand planes! / I hate flying!	J'ai horreur de l'avion ! (zhay o-rurr duh lav-ee-on)
I can't stand eating with my in-laws / I hate eating with my in-laws.	J'ai horreur de manger avec mes beaux-parents. (zhay o-rurr duh mon-zhay av-eck may boe pa-ron)
We can't stand eating with my parents / We hate eating with my parents.	Nous avons horreur de manger avec mes parents. (noo za-von o-rurr duh mon-zhay av-eck may pa-ron)
She can't stand working here / she hates working here.	Elle a horreur de travailler ici. (ell a o-rurr duh trav-eye-ay ee-see)

Well, that's it, you're done with Chapter 4! Remember, don't try to hold onto or remember anything you've learnt here. Everything you learnt in earlier chapters will be brought back up and reinforced in later chapters. You don't need to do anything or make any effort to memorise anything.

Use your "hidden moments"

A famous American linguist, Barry Farber, learnt a large part of the languages he spoke during the "hidden moments" he found in everyday life. Such hidden moments might include the time he would spend waiting for a train to arrive, time spent waiting for the kids to come out of school or for the traffic to get moving in the morning. These "hidden moments" would otherwise have been useless and unimportant in his daily life but, for someone learning a language, they were some of the most useful minutes of the day.

Breaking up your study time into lots of little bits like this can also help to stop it from feeling like a great effort, or from becoming impractical when your life gets especially hectic.

So, keep this book handy whenever you go out and then make use of such "hidden moments" whenever they come along.

CHAPTER 5

I was just about to order
a taxi when you called me.

I was just about to order a taxi when you called me.

Well, here we are again. Another chapter, beginning with another simple sentence: "I was just about to book a taxi when you called me."

This sentence has some very useful stuff in it and seems basic in English. But, as before, even if you know some French already, you may still struggle constructing it in French.

Okay, let's go!

What is "you have" (formal) in French?

Vous avez
(*voo* za-vay)

"Called" in French is:

appelé
(**a-play**)

So, how would you say "you have called"?

Vous avez appelé
(*voo* za-vay a-play)

And how would you say "you did call"?

Vous avez appelé
(*voo* za-vay a-play)

And "you called"?

Vous avez appelé
(*voo* za-vay a-play)

Once again you have three English past tenses for the price of one in French. Now, what is "you have" (informal)?

Tu as
(tü a)

How would you say "you have called", "you did call", "you called" (informal)?

Tu as appelé
(tü a a-play)

To recap, just on its own, what is "you have" (informal)?

Tu as
(tü a)

To say "you have me" (informal) in French, you will say:

Tu m'as
(tü ma)

So, literally this means, "you me have". Now, you might be wondering "When am I actually going to need to say 'you have me / you me have' in French?"

Well, if you want to say, for instance, "you called me" / "you did call me" / "you have called me" in French, then you will need to literally say "you me have called".

I'll show you how this works bit by bit just to make this clear.

Again, how would you say "you have" (informal)?

Tu as
(tü a)

And how would you say "you have me" (informal) – (literally "you me have")?

Tu m'as
(tü ma)

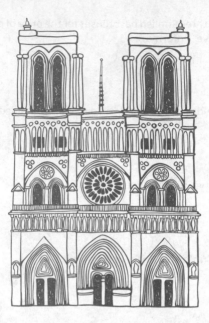

Let's add the word for "called" onto the end of this and by doing so you will say "you called me", "you did call me", "you have called me". So, do that now – say literally "you me have called":

Tu m'as appelé.
(tü ma a-play)

Let's try this now with "you have" (formal). First though, what is "you have" (formal)?

Vous avez
(voo za-vay)

"You have me" (formal) would be:

Vous m'avez
(voo ma-vay)

Again literally, this is "you me have."

So, how do you think you would say "you have called me", "you did call me", "you called me" (formal)?

Vous m'avez appelé.
(voo ma-vay a-play)

And again, how would you say "you have called me", "you did call me", "you called me" (informal)?

Tu m'as appelé.
(tü ma a-play)

"I was" in French is:

J'étais
(zhet-ay)

How would you say "I was romantic"?

J'étais romantique.
(zhet-ay roe-mon-teek)

"I was ironic"?

J'étais ironique.
(zhet-ay ee-ron-eek)

"I was critical"?

J'étais critique.
(zhet-ay krit-eek)

Time to steal some words!
Word Robbery Number 3

The third group of words we are going to steal are words that end in "**ary**" in English. These end in "**aire**" in French.

In this way, "ordin**ary**" becomes "ordin**aire**", "solit**ary**" becomes "solit**aire**", "contr**ary**" becomes "contr**aire**" and so on.

There are actually more than 400 of these in English and we can begin using these in French right away.

Adding them to the words we've already stolen so far, we have now reached a total of 2400 words stolen – and we're only on Chapter 5!

Words stolen so far 2400

So, how would you say "ordinary" in French?

ordinaire
(or-din-air)

And "I was ordinary"?

J'étais ordinaire.
(zhet-ay or-din-air)

How about "solitary"?

solitaire
(sol-it-air)

And "I was solitary"?

J'étais solitaire.
(zhet-ay sol-it-air)

You will find that "I was" really is a very useful phrase in French. Not only does it allow you to describe how you were but it also opens up some wonderful phrases for you.

For instance, to say "I was about to…" or "I was just about to…" in French, you will literally say "I was on the point of…", which is:

J'étais sur le point de…
(zhet-ay soor luh pwan duh)

What is "to reserve" or "to book" in French?

réserver
(ray-zurv-ay)

And what would be "to book a table"?

réserver une table
(ray-zurv-ay oon tarb-luh)

And again, what was "I was about to…" / "I was just about to…" (literally "I was on the point of…")?

J'étais sur le point de…
(zhet-ay soor luh pwan duh)

So, how would you say "I was about to book a table" (literally "I was on the point of to book a table")?

J'étais sur le point de réserver une table.
(zhet-ay soor luh pwan duh ray-zurv-ay oon tarb-luh)

What about "I was about to book a taxi"?

J'étais sur le point de réserver un taxi.
(zhet-ay soor luh pwan duh ray-zurv-ay urn taxi)

"To prepare" in French is:

préparer
(pray-par-ay)

So, what would be "to prepare the dinner"?

préparer le dîner
(pray-par-ay luh din-ay)

And how would you say "I was about to prepare the dinner":

J'étais sur le point de préparer le dîner.
(zhet-ay soor luh pwan duh pray-par-ay luh din-ay)

"To pay" is:

payer
(pay-ay)

How would you say "to pay the bill"?

payer l'addition
pay-ay la-dis-yon

Now try to say "I was about to pay the bill" (literally "I was on the point of to pay the bill"):

J'étais sur le point de payer l'addition.
(zhet-ay soor luh pwan duh pay-ay la-dis-yon)

And once more, how would you say "I was about to book a taxi"?

J'étais sur le point de réserver un taxi.
(zhet-ay soor luh pwan duh ray-zurv-ay urn taxi)

And again, what is "you have" (informal)?

Tu as
(tü a)

And "you have me" (informal)?

Tu m'as
(tü ma)

And how would you say "you have called me", "you did call me", "you called me" (informal) (literally "you me have called")?

Tu m'as appelé.
(tü ma a-play)

The word for "when" in French is:

quand
(kon)

So, how would you say "...when you called me" (informal)?

...quand tu m'as appelé.
(kon tü ma a-play)

How would you say "I was about to book a taxi"?

J'étais sur le point de réserver un taxi.
(zhet-ay soor luh pwan duh ray-zurv-ay urn taxi)

Let's put these two parts together now and say "I was about to book a taxi when you called me".

J'étais sur le point de réserver un taxi quand tu m'as appelé.
(zhet-ay soor luh pwan duh ray-zurv-ay urn taxi kon tü ma a-play)

Well done, another excellent sentence complete!

Building Blocks 5

Here they are:

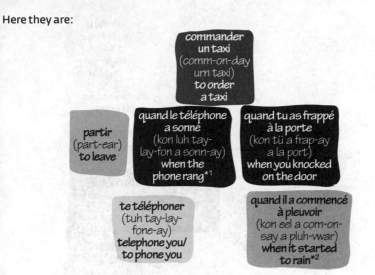

commander un taxi
(comm-on-day um taxi)
to order a taxi

partir
(part-ear)
to leave

quand le téléphone a sonné
(kon luh tay-lay-fon a sonn-ay)
when the phone rang*[1]

quand tu as frappé à la porte
(kon tü a frap-ay a la port)
when you knocked on the door

te téléphoner
(tuh tay-lay-fone-ay)
telephone you/ to phone you

quand il a commencé à pleuvoir
(kon eel a com-on-say a pluh-vwar)
when it started to rain*[2]

*[1] literally "when the telephone has sounded".

*[2] literally "when it has started to rain"

You know what to do!

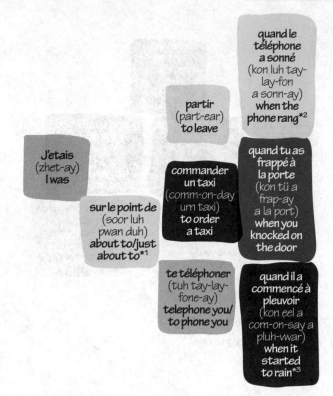

quand le téléphone a sonné
(kon luh tay-lay-fon a sonn-ay)
when the phone rang[2]

partir
(part-ear)
to leave

J'etais
(zhet-ay)
I was

commander un taxi
(comm-on-day urn taxi)
to order a taxi

quand tu as frappé à la porte
(kon tü a frap-ay a la port)
when you knocked on the door

sur le point de
(soor luh pwan duh)
about to/just about to[1]

te téléphoner
(tuh tay-lay-fone-ay)
telephone you/ to phone you

quand il a commencé à pleuvoir
(kon eel a com-on-say a pluh-vwar)
when it started to rain[3]

[1] literally "on the point of"

[2] literally "when the telephone has sounded"

[3] literally "when it has started to rain"

Another chapter finished, another checklist to go through. It's grown very long. Take your time with it. Remember, you don't need to do it all in one go.

le week-end (luh weekend)	the weekend
toxique (toks-eek)	toxic
statique (stat-eek)	static
sceptique (skept-eek)	sceptical
analytique (a-nal-ee-teek)	analytical
enthousiaste[6] (on-tooze-ee-ast)	enthusiastic
J'ai (zhay)	I have
visité (visit-ay)	visited
J'ai visité (zhay visit-ay)	I have visited / I visited / I did visit
Paris (pa-ree)	Paris
Notre-Dame (not-re darm)	Notre-Dame
J'ai visité Notre-Dame. (zhay visit-ay not-re darm)	I have visited Notre-Dame / I visited Notre-Dame / I did visit Notre-Dame.
passé (pass-ay)	spent
J'ai passé (zhay pass-ay)	I have spent / I spent / I did spend
Vous avez (voo za-vay)	You have
Vous avez passé (voo za-vay pass-ay)	You have spent / You spent / You did spend
Nous avons (noo za-von)	We have
Nous avons passé (noo za-von pass-ay)	We have spent / We spent / We did spend
septembre (sep-tom-bruh)	September
Noël (no-ell)	Christmas
à Paris (a pa-ree)	in Paris

---

6   In everything in life you will find exceptions to the rule and the same is true with these wonderful "ic" and "ical" Word Robberies. Although these conversions work almost all the time, "enthusiastic" is an exception to this technique that I would like you to learn. It's still an easy word to pick up, as it is so similar to the English, but it does not change in the way you would expect it to. I will leave it in the checklists from now on so that you learn it well.

en France (on fronce)	in France
en Suisse (on swees)	in Switzerland
Nous avons passé Noël en Suisse. (noo za-von pass-ay no-ell on swees)	We have spent Christmas in Switzerland / We spent Christmas in Switzerland / We did spend Christmas in Switzerland.
Vous avez passé septembre en France. (voo za-vay pass-ay sep-tom-bruh on fronce)	You have spent September in France / You spent September in France / You did spend September in France.
et (ay)	and
c'était (set-ay)	it was
C'était fantastique. (set-ay fon-tass-teek)	It was fantastic.
très agréable (trez ag-ray-arb-luh)	lovely / very agreeable
C'était très agréable. (set-ay trez ag-ray-arb-luh)	It was lovely. / It was very agreeable.
J'ai passé le week-end à Paris… et c'était très agréable. (zhay pass-ay luh weekend a pa-ree… ay set-ay trez ag-ray-arb-luh)	I spent the weekend in Paris… and it was lovely.
interprétation (an-turp-ray-tass-yon)	interpretation
observation (ob-sur-vass-yon)	observation
représentation (rep-ray-son-tass-yon)	representation
invité (earn-vit-ay)	invited
préparé (pray-par-ay)	prepared
réservé (ray-zurv-ay)	reserved / booked
commandé (comm-on-day)	ordered
payé (pay-ay)	paid
fait (fay)	done
l'addition (la-dis-yon)	the bill
le dîner (luh din-ay)	the dinner
le rosbif (luh ros-beef)	the roast beef

une table (oon tarb-luh)	a table
une chambre (oon shom-bruh)	a room
un taxi (urn taxi)	a taxi
J'ai préparé le dîner. (zhay pray-par-ay luh din-ay)	I have prepared the dinner / I prepared the dinner / I did prepare the dinner.
J'ai commandé le rosbif pour le dîner. (zhay comm-on-day luh ros-beef poor luh din-ay)	I have ordered roast beef for dinner / I ordered roast beef for dinner / I did order roast beef for dinner.
J'ai réservé une table pour vous. (zhay ray-zurv-ay oon tarb-luh poor voo)	I have booked a table for you / I booked a table for you / I did book a table for you.
Elle a (ell a)	She has
Elle a réservé une table pour ce soir. (ell a ray-zurv-ay oon tarb-luh poor sir swar)	She has booked / reserved a table for this evening – She booked / reserved a table for this evening – She did book / reserve a table for this evening.
Il a (eel a)	He has
Il a réservé une chambre pour deux personnes. (eel a ray-zurv-ay oon shom-bruh poor duh purse-on)	He has booked / reserved a room for two people – He booked / reserved a room for two people – He did book / reserve a room for two people.
Nous avons réservé un taxi pour vous. (noo za-von ray-zur-vay urn taxi poor voo)	We have booked a taxi for you / We booked a taxi for you / We did book a taxi for you.
Nous avons payé l'addition. (noo za-von pay-ay la-dis-yon)	We paid the bill / We have paid the the bill / We did pay the bill.
Qu'est-ce que ? (kess-kuh)	What? / What is it that?
Qu'est-ce que vous avez préparé ? (kess-kuh voo za-vay pray-par-ay)	What have you prepared? / What did you prepare? (literally "What is it that you have prepared?")
Qu'est-ce que vous avez fait ? (kess-kuh voo za-vay fay)	What have you done? / What did you do? (literally "What is it that you have done?")

J'ai réservé une table, commandé le dîner et puis payé l'addition. Qu'est-ce que vous avez fait ? (zhay ray-zurv-ay oon tarb-luh, comm-on-day luh din-ay ay pwee pay-ay la-dis-yon. kess-kuh voo za-vay fay)	I booked a table, ordered dinner and then paid the bill. What did you do?
J'ai l'intention de... (zhay lon-ton-syon duh)	I'm planning to... (literally "I have the intention of...")
J'ai l'intention de retourner en France en mai. (zhay lon-ton-syon duh ruh-toor-nay on fronce on mey)	I'm planning to go back to France in May.
J'ai peur de... (zhay purr duh)	I'm scared of... (literally "I have fear of...")
J'ai peur de retourner en France en septembre. (zhay purr duh ruh-toor-nay on fronce on sep-tom-bruh)	I'm scared of going back to France in September.
Vraiment ? (vray-mon)	Really?
alors (a-law)	so
mais (may)	but
J'ai envie de... (zhay on-vee duh)	I feel like... / I fancy... (literally "I have envy of...")
Oui, j'ai envie de retourner à Paris mais j'ai peur de l'avion, alors j'ai l'intention de prendre l'Eurostar. (wee zhay on-vee duh ruh-toor-nay a pa-ree may zhay purr duh lav-ee-on, a-law zhay lon-ton-syon duh pron-druh luh-roe-star)	Yes, I feel like going back to Paris but I'm scared of flying, so I'm planning to take the Eurostar.
J'ai envie d'acheter quelque chose ce matin. (zhay on-vee dash-tay kel-kuh shows sir mat-an)	I feel like / fancy buying something this morning.
Il a envie de lire quelque chose cet après-midi. (eel a on-vee duh leer kel-kuh shows set ap-ray mi-dee)	He feels like / fancies reading something this afternoon.
Ils ont (eel zon)	They have

Ils ont envie de manger quelque chose ce soir. (eel zon on-vee duh mon-zhay kel-kuh shows sir swar)	They feel like eating something this evening.
J'ai besoin de… (zhay burz-won duh)	I need… (literally "I have need of…")
J'ai besoin de parler français. (zhay burz-won duh par-lay fron-say)	I need to speak French.
J'ai besoin d'un taxi. (zhay burz-won durn taxi)	I need a taxi.
J'ai besoin d'une chambre. (zhay burz-won doon shom-bruh)	I need a room.
J'ai besoin d'aide. (zhay burz-won daid)	I need help.
Tu as besoin d'aide, mon pote ! (tü a burz-won daid mon pote)	You need help, mate!
J'ai horreur de… (zhay o-rurr duh)	I can't stand… / I hate… (literally "I have horror of…")
J'ai horreur de l'avion ! (zhay o-rurr duh lav-ee-on)	I can't stand flying! / I can't stand planes! / I hate flying!
J'ai horreur de manger avec mes beaux-parents. (zhay o-rurr duh mon-zhay av-eck may boe pa-ron)	I can't stand eating with my in-laws / I hate eating with my in-laws.
Nous avons horreur de manger avec mes parents. (noo za-von o-rurr duh mon-zhay av-eck may pa-ron)	We can't stand eating with my parents / We hate eating with my parents.
Elle a horreur de travailler ici. (ell a o-rurr duh trav-eye-ay ee-see)	She can't stand working here / she hates working here.
J'étais (zhet-ay)	I was
solitaire (sol-it-air)	solitary
contraire (kon-trair)	contrary
ordinaire (or-din-air)	ordinary
J'étais ordinaire. (zhet-ay or-din-air)	I was ordinary.
J'étais sur le point de… (zhet-ay soor luh pwan duh)	I was about to… / I was just about to… (literally "I was on the point of…")

J'étais sur le point de préparer le dîner. (zhet-ay soor luh pwan duh pray-par-ay luh din-ay)	I was about to prepare the dinner / I was just about to prepare the dinner.
J'étais sur le point de payer l'addition. (zhet-ay soor luh pwan duh pay-ay la-dis-yon)	I was about to pay the bill.[7]
J'étais sur le point de réserver une table. (zhet-ay soor luh pwan duh ray-zurv-ay oon tarb-luh)	I was just about to book a table.
Vous m'avez appelé. (voo ma-vay a-play)	You called me / You did call me / You have called me. (formal)
Tu m'as appelé. (tü ma a-play)	You called me / You did call me / You have called me. (informal)
quand (kon)	when
J'étais sur le point de réserver un taxi quand tu m'as appelé. (zhet-ay soor luh pwan duh ray-zurv-ay urn taxi kon tü ma a-play)	I was just about to book a taxi when you called me.
J'étais sur le point de partir quand le téléphone a sonné. (zhet-ay soor luh pwan duh part-ear kon luh tay-lay-fon a sonn-ay)	I was about to leave when the telephone rang.
J'étais sur le point de te téléphoner quand tu as frappé à la porte. (zhet-ay soor luh pwan duh tuh tay-lay-fone-ay kon tü a frap-ay a la port)	I was just about to phone you when you knocked at the door. (informal)
J'étais sur le point de commander un taxi quand il a commencé à pleuvoir. (zhet-ay soor luh pwan duh comm-on-day urn taxi kon deel a com-on-say a pluh-vwar)	I was just about to order a taxi when it started to rain.

---

7 All of the "sur le point de…" sentences here can be translated as "I was about to…" or "I was *just* about to…". Sometimes only one translation is given but, in all cases, you could translate it either way.

Okay, time for the other way round. Isn't it strange how translating French into English is much easier than translating English into French...?

the weekend	le week-end (luh weekend)
toxic	toxique (toks-eek)
static	statique (stat-eek)
sceptical	sceptique (skept-eek)
analytical	analytique (a-nal-ee-teek)
enthusiastic	enthousiaste (on-tooze-ee-ast)
I have	J'ai (zhay)
visited	visité (visit-ay)
I have visited / I visited / I did visit	J'ai visité (zhay visit-ay)
Paris	Paris (pa-ree)
Notre-Dame	Notre-Dame (not-re darm)
I have visited Notre-Dame / I visited Notre-Dame / I did visit Notre-Dame.	J'ai visité Notre-Dame. (zhay visit-ay not-re darm)
spent	passé (pass-ay)
I have spent / I spent / I did spend	J'ai passé (zhay pass-ay)
You have	Vous avez (voo za-vay)
You have spent / You spent / You did spend	Vous avez passé (voo za-vay pass-ay)
We have	Nous avons (noo za-von)
We have spent / We spent / We did spend	Nous avons passé (noo za-von pass-ay)
September	septembre (sep-tom-bruh)
Christmas	Noël (no-ell)
in Paris	à Paris (a pa-ree)
in France	en France (on fronce)
in Switzerland	en Suisse (on swees)
We have spent Christmas in Switzerland / We spent Christmas in Switzerland / We did spend Christmas in Switzerland.	Nous avons passé Noël en Suisse. (noo za-von pass-ay no-ell on swees)

You have spent September in France / You spent September in France / You did spend September in France.	**Vous avez passé septembre en France.** (voo za-vay pass-ay sep-tom-bruh on fronce)
and	**et** (ay)
it was	**c'était** (set-ay)
It was fantastic.	**C'était fantastique.** (set-ay fon-tass-teek)
lovely / very agreeable	**très agréable** (trez ag-ray-arb-luh)
It was lovely. / It was very agreeable.	**C'était très agréable.** (set-ay trez ag-ray-arb-luh)
I spent the weekend in Paris… and it was lovely.	**J'ai passé le week-end à Paris… et c'était très agréable.** (zhay pass-ay luh weekend a pa-ree… ay set-ay trez ag-ray-arb-luh)
interpretation	**interprétation** (an-turp-ray-tass-yon)
observation	**observation** (ob-sur-vass-yon)
representation	**représentation** (rep-ray-son-tass-yon)
invited	**invité** (earn-vit-ay)
prepared	**préparé** (pray-par-ay)
reserved / booked	**réservé** (ray-zurv-ay)
ordered	**commandé** (comm-on-day)
paid	**payé** (pay-ay)
done	**fait** (fay)
the bill	**l'addition** (la-dis-yon)
the dinner	**le dîner** (luh din-ay)
the roast beef	**le rosbif** (luh ros-beef)
a table	**une table** (oon tarb-luh)
a room	**une chambre** (oon shom-bruh)
a taxi	**un taxi** (urn taxi)
I have prepared the dinner / I prepared the dinner / I did prepare the dinner.	**J'ai préparé le dîner.** (zhay pray-par-ay luh din-ay)

I have ordered roast beef for dinner / I ordered roast beef for dinner / I did order roast beef for dinner.	**J'ai commandé le rosbif pour le dîner.** (zhay comm-on-day luh ros-beef poor luh din-ay)
I have booked a table for you / I booked a table for you / I did book a table for you.	**J'ai réservé une table pour vous.** (zhay ray-zurv-ay oon tarb-luh poor voo)
She has	**Elle a** (ell a)
She has booked / reserved a table for this evening – She booked / reserved a table for this evening – She did book / reserve a table for this evening.	**Elle a réservé une table pour ce soir.** (ell a ray-zurv-ay oon tarb-luh poor sir swar)
He has	**Il a** (eel a)
He has booked / reserved a room for two people – He booked / reserved a room for two people – He did book / reserve a room for two people.	**Il a réservé une chambre pour deux personnes.** (eel a ray-zurv-ay oon shom-bruh poor duh purse-on)
We have booked a taxi for you / We booked a taxi for you / We did book a taxi for you.	**Nous avons réservé un taxi pour vous.** (noo za-von ray-zur-vay urn taxi poor voo)
We paid the bill / We have paid the the bill / We did pay the bill.	**Nous avons payé l'addition.** (noo za-von pay-ay la-dis-yon)
What? / What is it that?	**Qu'est-ce que ?** (kess-kuh)
What have you prepared? / What did you prepare?	**Qu'est-ce que vous avez préparé ?** (kess-kuh voo za-vay pray-par-ay)
What have you done? / What did you do?	**Qu'est-ce que vous avez fait ?** (kess-kuh voo za-vay fay)
I booked a table, ordered dinner and then paid the bill. What did you do?	**J'ai réservé une table, commandé le dîner et puis payé l'addition. Qu'est-ce que vous avez fait ?** (zhay ray-zurv-ay oon tarb-luh, comm-on-day luh din-ay ay pwee pay-ay la-dis-yon. kess-kuh voo za-vay fay)
I'm planning to…	**J'ai l'intention de…** (zhay lon-ton-syon duh)

I'm planning to go back to France in May.	J'ai l'intention de retourner en France en mai. (zhay lon-ton-syon duh ruh-toor-nay on fronce on mey)
I'm scared of…	J'ai peur de… (zhay purr duh)
I'm scared of going back to France in September.	J'ai peur de retourner en France en septembre. (zhay purr duh ruh-toor-nay on fronce on sep-tom-bruh)
Really?	Vraiment ? (vray-mon)
so	alors (a-law)
but	mais (may)
I feel like… / I fancy…	J'ai envie de… (zhay on-vee duh)
Yes, I feel like going back to Paris but I'm scared of flying, so I'm planning to take the Eurostar.	Oui, j'ai envie de retourner à Paris mais j'ai peur de l'avion, alors j'ai l'intention de prendre l'Eurostar. (wee zhay on-vee duh ruh-toor-nay a pa-ree may zhay purr duh lav-ee-on, a-law zhay lon-ton-syon duh pron-druh luh-roe-star)
I feel like / fancy buying something this morning.	J'ai envie d'acheter quelque chose ce matin. (zhay on-vee dash-tay kel-kuh shows sir mat-an)
He feels like / fancies reading something this afternoon.	Il a envie de lire quelque chose cet après-midi. (eel a on-vee duh leer kel-kuh shows set ap-ray mi-dee)
They have	Ils ont (eel zon)
They feel like eating something this evening.	Ils ont envie de manger quelque chose ce soir. (eel zon on-vee duh mon-zhay kel-kuh shows sir swar)
I need…	J'ai besoin de… (zhay burz-won duh)
I need to speak French.	J'ai besoin de parler français. (zhay burz-won duh par-lay fron-say)
I need a taxi.	J'ai besoin d'un taxi. (zhay burz-won durn taxi)
I need a room.	J'ai besoin d'une chambre. (zhay burz-won doon shom-bruh)

I need help.	J'ai besoin d'aide. (zhay burz-won daid)
You need help, mate!	Tu as besoin d'aide, mon pote ! (tü a burz-won daid mon pote)
I can't stand… / I hate…	J'ai horreur de… (zhay o-rurr duh)
I can't stand flying! / I can't stand planes! / I hate flying!	J'ai horreur de l'avion ! (zhay o-rurr duh lav-ee-on)
I can't stand eating with my in-laws / I hate eating with my in-laws.	J'ai horreur de manger avec mes beaux-parents. (zhay o-rurr duh mon-zhay av-eck may boe pa-ron)
We can't stand eating with my parents / We hate eating with my parents.	Nous avons horreur de manger avec mes parents. (noo za-von o-rurr duh mon-zhay av-eck may pa-ron)
She can't stand working here / she hates working here.	Elle a horreur de travailler ici. (ell a o-rurr duh trav-eye-ay ee-see)
I was	J'étais (zhet-ay)
solitary	solitaire (sol-it-air)
contrary	contraire (kon-trair)
ordinary	ordinaire (or-din-air)
I was ordinary.	J'étais ordinaire. (zhet-ay or-din-air)
I was about to… / I was just about to… / (literally "I was on the point of…")	J'étais sur le point de… (zhet-ay soor luh pwan duh)
I was about to prepare the dinner / I was just about to prepare the dinner.	J'étais sur le point de préparer le dîner. (zhet-ay soor luh pwan duh pray-par-ay luh din-ay)
I was about to pay the bill.	J'étais sur le point de payer l'addition. (zhet-ay soor luh pwan duh pay-ay la-dis-yon)
I was just about to book a table.	J'étais sur le point de réserver une table. (zhet-ay soor luh pwan duh ray-zurv-ay oon tarb-luh)
You called me / You did call me / You have called me. (formal)	Vous m'avez appelé. (voo ma-vay a-play)
You called me / You did call me / You have called me. (informal)	Tu m'as appelé. (tü ma a-play)

when	quand (kon)
I was just about to book a taxi when you called me.	J'étais sur le point de réserver un taxi quand tu m'as appelé. (zhet-ay soor luh pwan duh ray-zurv-ay urn taxi kon tü ma a-play)
I was about to leave when the telephone rang.	J'étais sur le point de partir quand le téléphone a sonné. (zhet-ay soor luh pwan duh part-ear kon luh tay-lay-fon a sonn-ay)
I was just about to phone you when you knocked at the door. (informal)	J'étais sur le point de te téléphoner quand tu as frappé à la porte. (zhet-ay soor luh pwan duh tuh tay-lay-fone-ay kon tü a frap-ay a la port)
I was just about to order a taxi when it started to rain.	J'étais sur le point de commander un taxi quand il a commencé à pleuvoir. (zhet-ay soor luh pwan duh comm-on-day urn taxi kon deel a com-on-say a pluh-vwar)

That's it. Go and take your well-deserved break!

Forget what you were taught at school!

Many of us were told at school that we did not have an aptitude for languages, that we didn't have a "knack" or a "gift" for them.

Well, if this applies to you, then please let me assure you that this is all absolute nonsense! If you are able to read these words in front of you, then this demonstrates that you've been able to learn English. If you can learn one language, then your brain is just as capable of learning another – it simply needs to be approached in the right way.

In fact, if you've got as far as Chapter 5, it should already be obvious to you that you are quite capable of learning a foreign language when it's taught in the right way. The secret to success for you will be choosing the right materials once you've finished with this book (more on that later).

CHAPTER 6 (1)

I'm sorry, I was in the middle of preparing dinner when you arrived, so I was a bit distracted. (part 1)

> I'm sorry, I was in the middle of preparing dinner when you arrived, so I was a bit distracted.

Isn't it annoying when people turn up just as you're in the middle of something? And how much worse is it that you then need to apologise to them for ignoring them when they do?

Still, that's life, so you'd better get ready to deal with it in French!

So, remind me, how would you say "I have reserved", "I reserved", "I did reserve" in French?

J'ai réservé
(zhay ray-zurv-ay)

And how would you say "I have prepared," "I prepared", "I did prepare"?

J'ai préparé
(zhay pray-par-ay)

How about "I have paid", "I paid", "I did pay"?

J'ai payé
(zhay pay-ay)

And how would you say "you have paid", "you paid", "you did pay" (formal)?

Vous avez payé
(*voo* za-vay pay-ay)

And what about "you have paid", "you paid", "you did pay" (informal)?

Tu as payé
(tü a pay-ay)

As you learnt early on, in French you get three English past tenses for the price of one in French.

This means that by simply knowing how to say "I have...", "you have...", "we have..." and so on, you can express all three of these tenses, which is wonderful news for English speakers studying French.

However, it isn't entirely good news...

Although what I have said above is true in almost every instance in French, there is a set of words that work somewhat differently. These are words that, shall we say, come and go in a different way to the others. Let me explain.

Important comings and goings!

You already know that, when you want to use the past tense in French, you use "have".

So, to say "I reserved" in French you'll simply say "I *have* reserved", to say "you prepared" you'll say "you *have* prepared." You should be very used to this by now.

However, when you are talking about your comings and goings in French, you cannot use "have" to make the past tense.

So, for instance:

To say "I went" in French you will **not** say "I have gone"!

To say "I came" in French you will **not** say "I have come"!

To say "I left" in French (a type of going, I'm sure you'll agree) you will **not** say "I have left"!

And to say "I arrived" in French (a type of coming, I'm sure you'll also agree) you will **not** say "I have arrived"!

No, you cannot use "have" with these words, instead, strange as it sounds you will use "am".

So, for example:

To say "I went" you will say "I **am** gone"!

To say "I came" you will say "I **am** come"!

To say "I left" you will say "I **am** left"!

To say "I arrived" you will say "I **am** arrived"!

This sounds odd but, as I'll show you, it's something that's actually very easy to do. It's just an unfamiliar idea to us as English speakers, that's all!

Let me show you how this works in practice.

Let's imagine for a moment that I, the author, Paul Noble, have just arrived somewhere. And perhaps I decide to ring someone to tell them, very simply, that "I have arrived".

So, to begin with, the word I will use for "arrived" in French would be:

arrivé
(a-reev-ay)

Now, "I am" in French is:

je suis
(zhuh swee)

So, how would you say "I am arrived"?

Je suis arrivé.
(zhuh swee a-reev-ay)

And this means "I arrived", "I have arrived" and "I did arrive".

Notice that "I have" (J'ai) has not been used you will not use "have" when you are talking about your comings and goings.

Let's just check this again to make sure you have fully understood.

What is "I am" in French?

je suis
(zhuh swee)

And what is the word you have learnt for "arrived"?

arrivé
(a-reev-ay)

How would you say "I arrived"?

Je suis arrivé.
(zhuh swee a-reev-ay)

How about "I did arrive"?

Je suis arrivé.
(zhuh swee a-reev-ay)

And "I have arrived"?

Je suis arrivé.
(zhuh swee a-reev-ay)

Just as before, these are all the same in French, the only difference is that because arriving is a type of coming and going, you're not allowed to use "have" with it.

Also, before I forget, I should mention that there's something else to be aware of, something which affects how words like "arrived" are spelt in French. This is something I like to call the Fiancé Rule.

The Fiancé Rule

You may well be thinking, "what on earth is this?" Well, we all know what a fiancé is, don't we? It's a person someone is engaged to. And, in English, when it's a male person you are engaged to, the word is spelt "fiancé". However, when it's a female person you're engaged to, it's spelt "fiancée" with an extra "e" on the end.

This fiancé / fiancée rule is something that is used in French whenever you create the past tense using "am". Let's look at an example to make this easier to understand.

As I've already said, if I, the author (and I'm a guy) were to say "I have arrived", you would write it as:

Je suis arrivé.
(zhuh swee a-reev-ay)

But if a woman said the same thing, it would be written like this instead:

Je suis arrivée.
(zhuh swee a-reev-ay)

So you can see how, although it is "arrivé" for a man who has arrived, it is by contrast "arrivée" for a woman, with an extra "e" on the end. This is just how the words "fiancé" and "fiancée" work in English – "fiancé" for a man but "fiancée", with an extra "e", for a woman.

As I've said though, this only applies when you are talking about your comings and goings, that is, when you use "am" instead of "have" to make the past tense.

When you use "have" to make the past tense (which is what you normally do), the spelling doesn't change; take a look:

I have reserved (said by a man)	J'ai réservé. (zhay ray-zurv-ay)
I have reserved (said by a woman)	J'ai réservé. (zhay ray-zurv-ay)

You see? They are the same – and they never change!

However, when a man or woman is talking about going or coming or arriving or leaving, then it does change.

"Gone" referring to a man in French is:

allé
(al-ay)

So, how would a man say "I have gone",
"I went", "I did go" (literally "I am gone")?

Je suis allé.
(zhuh swee zal-ay)

How do you think it would be spelt if a woman
were to say "I have gone", "I went", "I did go"
(literally "I am gone")?

Je suis allée.
(zhuh swee zal-ay)

Look, there's that extra "e" on the end!

It's important to be aware that this doesn't affect the pronunciation, so this spelling change won't affect you when you're speaking. However, as your ability in French develops you will need to have some understanding of what causes the spelling changes that you will sometimes see in French. If you don't, you are likely to feel totally baffled as to why a word seems to be spelt one way one minute and another way the next!

Now, I've told you that instead of saying "I have arrived" in French, you will literally say "I am arrived" and that instead of saying "I have gone" in French, you'll literally say "I am gone."

Well, the same logic applies to when you are saying "he", "she", "you", "we", "they" went, arrived, have gone and so on.

So, for example:

If you want to say "he has gone", you'll literally say "he is gone".

If you want to say "she has gone", you'll literally say "she is gone".

If you want to say "you have gone", you'll literally say "you are gone".

"You are" (formal) in French is:

Vous êtes
(*voo zet*)

So, how do you think you would say "you have gone" (formal) when you're talking **to a man**?

Vous êtes allé.
(*voo zet al-ay*)

And how do you think it would be written if you said it **to a woman**?

Vous êtes allée.
(*voo zet al-ay*)

And how do you think you would say "you have arrived", "you arrived", "you did arrive" (formal) when talking **to a man**?

Vous êtes arrivé.
(*voo zet a-reev-ay*)

And how would this look if it was said **to a woman**?

Vous êtes arrivée.
(*voo zet a-reev-ay*)

So, this change in how it's written applies both when someone is saying it about themselves and when you are saying it about someone else. It changes based on the gender of the person being described.

"You are" (informal) in French is:

Tu es
(*tü ay*)

So, how would you say to a woman
"you have arrived", "you arrived",
"you did arrive" (informal)?

Tu es arrivée.
(*tü ay a-reev-ay*)

And how would that look if it was said to a man?

Tu es arrivé.
(tü ay a-reev-ay)

Okay, let's just leave it at that for the moment. When you're ready, you can go on to the next chapter and you can complete the sentence. But before you do that, feel free to read through this chapter a few times, practising the sentence-building. That will help you become comfortable with this aspect of French.

As I have already said, the spelling changes explained above by the Fiancé Rule won't affect you when you speak. It is, however, very useful to know why the spelling of certain French words seems to change from time to time.

And by the way, if you want a quick summary of what you really need to grasp from this chapter, the three key points that I want you to take from it are:

1. The Fiancé Rule only affects words to do with your comings and goings (go, come, arrive, leave). For other words, like when you want to say you've booked or paid for or ordered something, just use "have" to make the past tense (like you did at the start of this book).

2. When you are talking about your comings and goings, however, you do need to use "am" or "is" or "are" when you want to say that someone has arrived, gone, come or left. So, you say "I *am* arrived" not "I *have* arrived", and you say "you *are* gone" not "you *have* gone". I know it seems weird – just try to accept it!

3. The words for "arrived", "went", "came" or "left" in French will have an "e" added onto them when they are describing someone female. This doesn't affect the pronunciation.

That's it. If you've more or less got those points, then you're ready to move on.

CHAPTER 6 (2)

I'm sorry, I was in the middle of preparing dinner when you arrived, so I was a bit distracted. (part 2)

> I'm sorry, I was in the middle of preparing dinner when you arrived, so I was a bit distracted.

Alright, now that you're aware of the Fiancé Rule and why the spelling sometimes changes in French, let's get back to building this sentence.

So again, how would you say "I was about to..." (literally "I was on the point of") in French?

J'étais sur le point de...
(zhet-ay soor luh pwan duh)

And how would you say "I was about to book a taxi"?

J'étais sur le point de réserver un taxi.
(zhet-ay soor luh pwan duh ray-zurv-ay urn taxi)

How about "I was about to pay the bill"?

J'étais sur le point de payer l'addition.
(zhet-ay soor luh pwan duh pay-ay la-dis-yon)

And "I was about to prepare the dinner"?

J'étais sur le point de préparer le dîner.
(zhet-ay soor luh pwan duh pray-par-ay luh din-ay)

You should now be quite familiar with this phrase "I was about to..." and it's certainly very useful.

There is another similarly structured phrase in French, which is also equally useful, which means "I was in the middle of..."

To say "I was in the middle of..." in French, you will literally say "I was in train of..." This is somewhat similar to the way in which, in English, we might talk about being in the middle of a train of thought.

So, "I was in the middle of…" in French is literally "I was in train of…" which in French is:

J'étais en train de…
(zhet-ay on tran duh)

How would you say "I was in the middle of preparing the dinner" (literally "I was in train of to prepare the dinner")?

J'étais en train de préparer le dîner.
(zhet-ay on tran duh pray-par-ay luh din-ay)

How about "I was in the middle of paying the bill"?

J'étais en train de payer l'addition.
(zhet-ay on tran duh pay-ay la-dis-yon)

And "I was in the middle of booking a taxi"?

J'étais en train de réserver un taxi.
(zhct-ay on tran duh ray-zurv-ay urn taxi)

What is "to eat"?

manger
(mon-zhay)

So, how would you say "I was in the middle of eating" (literally "I was in train of to eat")?

J'étais en train de manger.
(zhet-ay on tran duh mon-zhay)

And again, how would a man say "I have arrived", "I arrived", "I did arrive" in French (literally "I am arrived")?

Je suis arrivé.
(zhuh swee a-reev-ay)

What about a woman?

Je suis arrivée.
(zhuh swee a-reev-ay)

coffee

Keep in mind that these are pronounced in exactly the same way as one another but that there is a spelling change that works according to the Fiancé Rule.

Now, how would you say to a man (formal): "you have arrived", "you arrived", "you did arrive"?

Vous êtes arrivé.
(voo zet a-reev-ay)

How about to a woman (formal): "you have arrived", "you arrived", "you did arrive"?

Vous êtes arrivée.
(voo zet a-reev-ay)

And what about to a woman (informal): "you have arrived", "you arrived", "you did arrive"?

Tu es arrivée.
(tü ay a-reev-ay)

And how would you say the same to a man (informal) "you have arrived", "you arrived", "you did arrive"?

Tu es arrivé.
(tü ay a-reev-ay)

You can see that there are differences in the spelling here that follow the Fiancé Rule but they do not affect the pronunciation.

What is the word for "when" in French?

Quand
(kon)

So, how would you say "...when you arrived" (informal)?

...quand tu es arrivé / arrivée.[8]
(kon tü ay a-reev-ay)

---

[8]   From now on, both spelling possibilities for whether you were talking to a man or a woman will be included in the answer. As the pronunciation is identical for both, the spelling change wouldn't affect spoken French anyway. If you want to write in French, however, just remember that the one with the additional "e" on the end is what you use when describing something feminine.

How would you say "I was in the middle of…"?

J'étais en train de…
(zhet-ay on tran duh)

What about "I was in the middle of preparing the dinner"?

J'étais en train de préparer le dîner.
(zhet-ay on tran duh pray-par-ay luh din-ay)

And "I was in the middle of eating"?

J'étais en train de manger.
(zhet-ay on tran duh mon-zhay)

How about "I was in the middle of eating when you arrived" (informal)?

J'étais en train de manger quand tu es arrivé / arrivée.
(zhet-ay on tran duh mon-zhay kon tü ay a-reev-ay)

And "I was in the middle of preparing the dinner when you arrived" (informal)?

J'étais en train de préparer le dîner quand tu es arrivé / arrivée.
(zhet-ay on tran duh pray-par-ay luh din-ay kon tü ay a-reev-ay)

Again, what is "I am" in French?

Je suis
(zhuh swee)

The word for "sorry" in French is spelt "désolé" (dez-oh-lay) if you are a man and "désolée" (dez-oh-lay) if you're a woman.

Now that you know this, how would you say "I'm sorry" in French?

Je suis désolé / désolée.
(zhuh swee dez-oh-lay)

And how would you say "I'm sorry, I was in the middle of preparing the dinner when you arrived" (informal)?

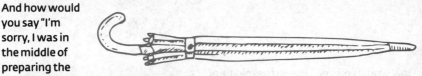

Je suis désolé / désolée, j'étais en train de préparer le dîner quand tu es arrivé / arrivée.
(zhuh swee dez-oh-lay, zhet-ay on tran duh pray-par-ay luh din-ay kon tü ay a-reev-ay)

And how would you say "I'm sorry, I was in the middle of eating when you arrived" (informal)?

Je suis désolé / désolée, j'étais en train de manger quand tu es arrivé / arrivée.
(zhuh swee dez-oh-lay, zhet-ay on tran duh mon-zhay kon tü ay a-reev-ay)

Now, once more, just on its own, what is "I was" in French?

J'étais
(zhet-ay)

So, how would you say "I was romantic"?

J'étais romantique.
(zhet-ay roe-mon-teek)

And once more, what is the word for "so" in French?

alors
(a-law)

It's worth pointing out that in English we actually use "so" to mean more than one thing. For instance, we can say "I liked the jacket, so I bought it" or "I'm not happy here, so I'm leaving." It's sort of a less formal way of saying "therefore" – "I like the jacket, therefore I bought it", "I'm not happy here, therefore I'm leaving." It would, of course, sound strange to use "therefore" in these situations because it sounds a bit too formal – but the meaning is essentially the same.

Anyway, this is the type of "so" that you have been using "alors" to express in French, the "so" that is a less formal way of saying "therefore". This is the kind of "so" you would use in the examples I've just given, or to say something like "I'm tired, so I'm going to bed."

There is, however, another way in which we use "so" in English. This "so" is used, for instance, when we say "I was so happy", "I was so excited", or "he's so romantic". This "so" clearly doesn't mean "therefore". Its meaning is more like "very" or "extremely".

The word for this type of "so" in French is:

tellement
(tel-mon)

So, how would you say:

"I was so enthusiastic"?

J'étais tellement enthousiaste.
(zhet-ay tel-mon on-tooze-ee-ast)

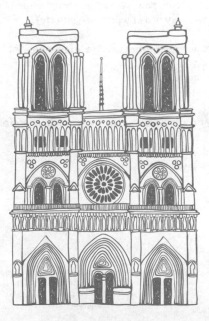

One way to say you're distracted in French is to say that you are "preoccupied". "Preoccupied" in French is:

préoccupé / préoccupée[9]
(pray-ok-oo-pay)

So, how would you say "I was so distracted", "I was so preoccupied"?

J'étais tellement préoccupé / préoccupée.
(zhet-ay tel-mon pray-ok-oo-pay)

And now let's take away the "so" and say simply "I was distracted?"

J'étais préoccupé / préoccupée.
(zhet-ay pray-ok-oo-pay)

"A bit" or "a little" in French is:

un peu
(urn puh)

How would you say "I was a bit distracted", "I was a little preoccupied"?

J'étais un peu préoccupé / préoccupée.
(zhet-ay urn peu pray-ok-oo-pay)

Now again, what was "so" in the sense of "extremely" or "very" in French?

tellement
(tel-mon)

And what was "so" in the sense of "therefore"?

alors
(a-law)

---

9   You'll notice that here there are two spellings for "preoccupied". One is for someone male, the other (with the extra "e" on the end) for someone female. This is the Fiancé Rule at work again, this time affecting a describing word. Again, this isn't something to worry about, but I just want to point it out in case you wonder again why the spelling sometimes changes in French.

So, how would you say "...so I was a bit distracted", "... so I was a little preoccupied", meaning "...therefore I was a little preoccupied"?

...alors j'étais un peu préoccupé / préoccupée.
(a-law zhet-ay urn peu pray-ok-oo-pay)

And again, how would you say "I'm sorry"?

Je suis désolé / désolée.
(zhuh swee dez-oh-lay)

And what was "I was in the middle of..."?

J'étais en train de...
(zhet-ay on tran duh)

Okay, how would you say "I'm sorry, I was in the middle of eating when you arrived" (informal) (literally "I'm sorry, I was in train of to eat when you arrived")?

Je suis désolé / désolée, j'étais en train de manger quand tu es arrivé / arrivée.
(zhuh swee dez-oh-lay, zhet-ay on tran duh mon-zhay kon tü ay a-reev-ay)

What about, "I'm sorry, I was in the middle of preparing dinner when you arrived" (informal)?

Je suis désolé / désolée, j'étais en train de préparer le dîner quand tu es arrivé / arrivée.
(zhuh swee dez-oh-lay, zhet-ay on tran duh pray-par-ay luh din-ay kon tü ay a-reev-ay)

Finally, let's imagine you had been preparing a dinner for some special guests when your friend came over to see you. To explain your mood you wanted to say "I'm sorry, I was in the middle of preparing dinner when you arrived, so I was a bit distracted / preoccupied." (informal):

Je suis désolé / désolée, j'étais en train de préparer le dîner quand tu es arrivé / arrivée, alors j'étais un peu préoccupé / préoccupée.
(zhuh swee dez-oh-lay, zhet-ay on tran duh pray-par-ay luh din-ay kon tü ay a-reev-ay, a-law zhet-ay urn peu pray-ok-oo-pay)

Well done with that! Again, take your time practising that last sentence until you feel confident constructing it. There's never a need to rush on to the next section until you feel you have properly finished with the previous one.

Sixth chapter, six new building blocks:

t'appeler
(tapp-lay)
**calling you/
to call you**

t'écrire
(tay kreer)
**writing to
you/to write
to you**

quand ta lettre
ést arrivée
(kon ta let-ruh ay
ta-reev-ay)
**when your letter
arrived**[1]

quand tu m'as
téléphoné
(kon tü ma
tay-lay-fone-ay)
**when you
phoned me**

quand ma mère
est arrivée
(kon ma maire
ay ta-reev-ay)
**when my mother
arrived**[2]

partir de la maison
(part-ear duh
la may-zon)
**leaving the
house/to leave
the house**

[1] literally "when your letter is arrived"

[2] literally "when my mother is arrived"

Now build me some sentences, please!

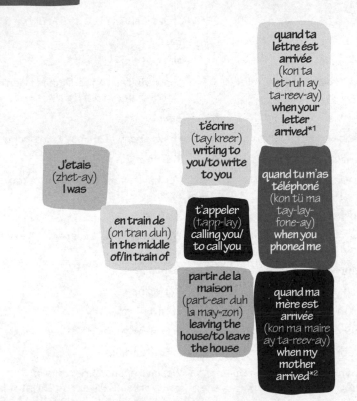

quand ta lettre est arrivée (kon ta let-ruh ay ta-reev-ay) **when your letter arrived***1

t'écrire (tay kreer) **writing to you/to write to you**

J'etais (zhet-ay) **I was**

quand tu m'as téléphoné (kon tü ma tay-lay-fone-ay) **when you phoned me**

en train de (on tran duh) **in the middle of/in train of**

t'appeler (tapp-lay) **calling you/ to call you**

partir de la maison (part-ear duh la may-zon) **leaving the house/to leave the house**

quand ma mère est arrivée (kon ma maire ay ta-reev-ay) **when my mother arrived***2

*1 literally "when your letter is arrived"

*2 literally "when my mother is arrived"

Checklist number 6, take your time and enjoy it (if you can)!

le week-end (luh weekend)	the weekend
diabétique (dee-ah-bet-eek)	diabetic
asthmatique (ass-mat-eek)	asthmatic
fanatique (fan-at-eek)	fanatical

satirique (sat-ear-eek)	satirical
enthousiaste (on-tooze-ee-ast)	enthusiastic
J'ai (zhay)	I have
visité (visit-ay)	visited
J'ai visité (zhay visit-ay)	I have visited / I visited / I did visit
Paris (pa-ree)	Paris
Notre-Dame (not-re darm)	Notre-Dame
J'ai visité Notre-Dame. (zhay visit-ay not-re darm)	I have visited Notre-Dame / I visited Notre-Dame / I did visit Notre-Dame.
passé (pass-ay)	spent
J'ai passé (zhay pass-ay)	I have spent / I spent / I did spend
Vous avez (voo za-vay)	You have
Vous avez passé (voo za-vay pass-ay)	You have spent / You spent / You did spend
Nous avons (noo za-von)	We have
Nous avons passé (noo za-von pass-ay)	We have spent / We spent / We did spend
septembre (sep-tom-bruh)	September
Noël (no-ell)	Christmas
à Paris (a pa-ree)	in Paris
en France (on fronce)	in France
en Suisse (on swees)	in Switzerland
Nous avons passé Noël en Suisse. (noo za-von pass-ay no-ell on swees)	We have spent Christmas in Switzerland / We spent Christmas in Switzerland / We did spend Christmas in Switzerland.
Vous avez passé septembre en France. (voo za-vay pass-ay sep-tom-bruh on fronce)	You have spent September in France / You spent September in France / You did spend September in France.
et (ay)	and
c'était (set-ay)	it was
C'était fantastique. (set-ay fon-tass-teek)	It was fantastic.
très agréable (trez ag-ray-arb-luh)	lovely / very agreeable

C'était très agréable. (set-ay trez ag-ray-arb-luh)	It was lovely. / It was very agreeable.
J'ai passé le week-end à Paris... et c'était très agréable. (zhay pass-ay luh weekend a pa-ree... ay set-ay trez ag-ray-arb-luh)	I spent the weekend in Paris... and it was lovely.
obligation (ob-lig-ass-yon)	obligation
négociation (nay-gos-ee-ass-yon)	negotiation
détermination (day-term-in-ass-yon)	determination
invité (earn-vit-ay)	invited
préparé (pray-par-ay)	prepared
réservé (ray-zurv-ay)	reserved / booked
commandé (comm-on-day)	ordered
payé (pay-ay)	paid
fait (fay)	done
l'addition (la-dis-yon)	the bill
le dîner (luh din-ay)	the dinner
le rosbif (luh ros-beef)	the roast beef
une table (oon tarb-luh)	a table
une chambre (oon shom-bruh)	a room
un taxi (urn taxi)	a taxi
J'ai préparé le dîner. (zhay pray-par-ay luh din-ay)	I have prepared the dinner / I prepared the dinner / I did prepare the dinner.
J'ai commandé le rosbif pour le dîner. (zhay comm-on-day luh ros-beef poor luh din-ay)	I have ordered roast beef for dinner / I ordered roast beef for dinner / I did order roast beef for dinner.
J'ai réservé une table pour vous. (zhay ray-zurv-ay oon tarb-luh poor voo)	I have booked a table for you / I booked a table for you / I did book a table for you.
Elle a (ell a)	She has
Elle a réservé une table pour ce soir. (ell a ray-zurv-ay oon tarb-luh poor sir swar)	She has booked / reserved a table for this evening – She booked / reserved a table for this evening – She did book / reserve a table for this evening.

Il a (eel a)	He has
Il a réservé une chambre pour deux personnes. (eel a ray-zurv-ay oon shom-bruh poor duh purse-on)	He has booked / reserved a room for two people – He booked / reserved a room for two people – He did book / reserve a room for two people.
Nous avons réservé un taxi pour vous. (noo za-von ray-zur-vay urn taxi poor voo)	We have booked a taxi for you / We booked a taxi for you / We did book a taxi for you.
Nous avons payé l'addition. (noo za-von pay-ay la-dis-yon)	We paid the bill / We have paid the the bill / We did pay the bill.
Qu'est-ce que ? (kess-kuh)	What? / What is it that?
Qu'est-ce que vous avez préparé ? (kess-kuh voo za-vay pray-par-ay)	What have you prepared? / What did you prepare? (literally "What is it that you have prepared?")
Qu'est-ce que vous avez fait ? (kess-kuh voo za-vay fay)	What have you done? / What did you do? (literally "What is it that you have done?")
J'ai réservé une table, commandé le dîner et puis payé l'addition. Qu'est-ce que vous avez fait ? (zhay ray-zurv-ay oon tarb-luh, comm-on-day luh din-ay ay pwee pay-ay la-dis-yon. kess-kuh voo za-vay fay)	I booked a table, ordered dinner and then paid the bill. What did you do?
J'ai l'intention de... (zhay lon-ton-syon duh)	I'm planning to... (literally "I have the intention of...")
J'ai l'intention de retourner en France en mai. (zhay lon-ton-syon duh ruh-toor-nay on fronce on mey)	I'm planning to go back to France in May.
J'ai peur de... (zhay purr duh)	I'm scared of... (literally "I have fear of...")
J'ai peur de retourner en France en septembre. (zhay purr duh ruh-toor-nay on fronce on sep-tom-bruh)	I'm scared of going back to France in September.
Vraiment ? (vray-mon)	Really?
alors (a-law)	so (therefore)
mais (may)	but

J'ai envie de… (zhay on-vee duh)	I feel like… / I fancy… (literally "I have envy of…")
Oui, j'ai envie de retourner à Paris mais j'ai peur de l'avion, alors j'ai l'intention de prendre l'Eurostar. (wee zhay on-vee duh ruh-toor-nay a pa-ree may zhay purr duh lav-ee-on, a-law zhay lon-ton-syon duh pron-druh luh-roe-star)	Yes, I feel like going back to Paris but I'm scared of flying, so I'm planning to take the Eurostar.
J'ai envie d'acheter quelque chose ce matin. (zhay on-vee dash-tay kel-kuh shows sir mat-an)	I feel like / fancy buying something this morning.
Il a envie de lire quelque chose cet après-midi. (eel a on-vee duh leer kel-kuh shows set ap-ray mi-dee)	He feels like / fancies reading something this afternoon.
Ils ont (eel zon)	They have
Ils ont envie de manger quelque chose ce soir. (eel zon on-vee duh mon-zhay kel-kuh shows sir swar)	They feel like eating something this evening.
J'ai besoin de… (zhay burz-won duh)	I need… (literally "I have need of…")
J'ai besoin de parler français. (zhay burz-won duh par-lay fron-say)	I need to speak French.
J'ai besoin d'un taxi. (zhay burz-won durn taxi)	I need a taxi.
J'ai besoin d'une chambre. (zhay burz-won doon shom-bruh)	I need a room.
J'ai besoin d'aide. (zhay burz-won daid)	I need help.
Tu as besoin d'aide, mon pote ! (tü a burz-won daid mon pote)	You need help, mate!
J'ai horreur de… (zhay o-rurr duh)	I can't stand… / I hate… (literally "I have horror of…")
J'ai horreur de l'avion ! (zhay o-rurr duh lav-ee-on)	I can't stand flying! / I can't stand planes! / I hate flying!
J'ai horreur de manger avec mes beaux-parents. (zhay o-rurr duh manger av-eck may boe pa-ron)	I can't stand eating with my in-laws / I hate eating with my in-laws.

Nous avons horreur de manger avec mes parents. (noo za-von o-rurr duh mon-zhay av-eck may pa-ron)	We can't stand eating with my parents / We hate eating with my parents.
Elle a horreur de travailler ici. (ell a o-rurr duh trav-eye-ay ee-see)	She can't stand working here / she hates working here.
J'étais (zhet-ay)	I was
nécessaire (nay-sess-air)	necessary
secrétaire (sek-ray-taire)	secretary
salaire (sal-air)	salary
J'étais ordinaire. (zhet-ay or-din-air)	I was ordinary.
J'étais sur le point de… (zhet-ay soor luh pwan duh)	I was about to… / I was just about to… (literally "I was on the point of…")
J'étais sur le point de préparer le dîner. (zhet-ay soor luh pwan duh pray-par-ay luh din-ay)	I was about to prepare the dinner / I was just about to prepare the dinner.
J'étais sur le point de payer l'addition. (zhet-ay soor luh pwan duh pay-ay la-dis-yon)	I was about to pay the bill.
J'étais sur le point de réserver une table. (zhet-ay soor luh pwan duh ray-zurv-ay oon tarb-luh)	I was just about to book a table.
Vous m'avez appelé. (voo ma-vay a-play)	You called me / You did call me / You have called me. (formal)
Tu m'as appelé. (tü ma a-play)	You called me / You did call me / You have called me. (informal)
quand (kon)	when
J'étais sur le point de réserver un taxi quand tu m'as appelé. (zhet-ay soor luh pwan duh ray-zurv-ay urn taxi kon tü ma a-play)	I was just about to book a taxi when you called me.
J'étais sur le point de partir quand le téléphone a sonné. (zhet-ay soor luh pwan duh part-ear kon luh tay-lay-fon a sonn-ay)	I was about to leave when the telephone rang.

J'étais sur le point de te téléphoner quand tu as frappé à la porte. (zhet-ay soor luh pwan duh tuh tay-lay-fone-ay kon tü a frap-ay a la port)	I was just about to phone you when you knocked at the door. (informal)
J'étais sur le point de commander un taxi quand il a commencé à pleuvoir. (zhet-ay soor luh pwan duh comm-on-day urn taxi kon deel a com-on-say a pluh-vwar)	I was just about to order a taxi when it started to rain.
tellement (tel-mon)	so (extremely, very)
je suis (zhuh swee)	I am
arrivé / arrivée (a-reev-ay)	arrived
Je suis arrivé. (zhuh swee a-reev-ay)	I have arrived / I arrived / I did arrive. (said by a man / boy)
Je suis arrivée. (zhuh swee a-reev-ay)	I have arrived / I arrived / I did arrive. (said by a woman / girl)
allé / allée (al-ay)	gone
Je suis allé. (zhuh swee zal-ay)	I have gone / I went / I did go. (said by a man / boy)
Je suis allée. (zhuh swee zal-ay)	I have gone / I went / I did go. (said by a woman / girl)
Vous êtes (voo zet)	You are (formal)
Vous êtes allé. (voo zet al-ay)	You have gone / You went / You did go. (said to a man / boy) – formal
Vous êtes allée. (voo zet al-ay)	You have gone / You went / You did go. (said to a woman / girl) – formal
Vous êtes arrivé. (voo zet a-reev-ay)	You have arrived / You arrived / You did arrive. (said to a man / boy) – formal
Vous êtes arrivée. (voo zet a-reev-ay)	You have arrived / You arrived / You did arrive. (said to a woman / girl) – formal
Tu es (tü ay)	You are (informal)
Tu es arrivé. (tü ay a-reev-ay)	You have arrived / You arrived / You did arrive. (said to a man / boy) – informal

Tu es arrivée. (tü ay a-reev-ay)	You have arrived / You arrived / You did arrive. (said to a woman / girl) – informal
Je suis désolé / désolée. (zhuh swee dez-oh-lay)	I'm sorry.
un peu (urn puh)	a little / a bit
J'étais un peu préoccupé / préoccupée. (zhet-ay urn puh pray-ok-oo-pay)	I was a little preoccupied / distracted.
J'étais en train de… (zhet-ay on tran duh)	I was in the middle of… (literally "I was in train of…")
Je suis désolé / désolée, j'étais en train de manger quand tu es arrivé / arrivée. (zhuh swee dez-oh-lay, zhet-ay on tran duh mon-zhay kon tü ay a-reev-ay)	I'm sorry, I was in the middle of eating when you arrived. (informal)
Je suis désolé / désolée, j'étais en train de préparer le dîner quand tu es arrivé / arrivée, alors j'étais un peu préoccupé / préoccupée. (zhuh swee dez-oh-lay, zhet-ay on tran duh pray-par-ay luh din-ay kon tü ay a-reev-ay a-law zhet-ay urn puh pray-ok-oo-pay)	I'm sorry, I was in the middle of preparing dinner when you arrived so I was a bit distracted. (informal)
J'étais en train de t'écrire quand ma mère est arrivée. (zhet-ay on tran duh tay kreer kon ma maire ay ta-reev-ay)	I was in the middle of writing to you when my mother arrived. (informal)
J'étais en train de partir de la maison quand tu m'as téléphoné. (zhet-ay on tran duh part-ear duh la may-zon kon tü ma tay-lay-fone-ay)	I was in the middle of leaving the house when you phoned me. (informal)
J'étais en train de t'appeler quand ta lettre est arrivée. (zhet-ay on tran duh tap-lay kon ta let-ruh ay ta-reev-ay)	I was in the middle of calling you when your letter arrived. (informal)

Now enjoy yourself doing it the other way round.

Twice the fun for half the effort... erm... kind of.

the weekend	le week-end (luh weekend)
diabetic	diabétique (dee-ah-bet-eek)
asthmatic	asthmatique (ass-mat-eek)
fanatical	fanatique (fan-at-eek)
satirical	satirique (sat-ear-eek)
enthusiastic	enthousiaste (on-tooze-ee-ast)
I have	J'ai (zhay)
visited	visité (visit-ay)
I have visited / I visited / I did visit	J'ai visité (zhay visit-ay)
Paris	Paris (pa-ree)
Notre-Dame	Notre-Dame (not-re darm)
I have visited Notre-Dame / I visited Notre-Dame / I did visit Notre-Dame.	J'ai visité Notre-Dame. (zhay visit-ay not-re darm)
spent	passé (pass-ay)
I have spent / I spent / I did spend	J'ai passé (zhay pass-ay)
You have	Vous avez (voo za-vay)
You have spent / You spent / You did spend	Vous avez passé (voo za-vay pass-ay)
We have	Nous avons (noo za-von)
We have spent / We spent / We did spend	Nous avons passé (noo za-von pass-ay)
September	septembre (sep-tom-bruh)
Christmas	Noël (no-ell)
in Paris	à Paris (a pa-ree)
in France	en France (on fronce)
in Switzerland	en Suisse (on swees)
We have spent Christmas in Switzerland / We spent Christmas in Switzerland / We did spend Christmas in Switzerland.	Nous avons passé Noël en Suisse. (noo za-von pass-ay no-ell on swees)

You have spent September in France / You spent September in France / You did spend September in France.	Vous avez passé septembre en France. (voo za-vay pass-ay sep-tom-bruh on fronce)
and	et (ay)
it was	c'était (set-ay)
It was fantastic.	C'était fantastique. (set-ay fon-tass-teek)
lovely / very agreeable	très agréable (trez ag-ray-arb-luh)
It was lovely. / It was very agreeable.	C'était très agréable. (set-ay trez ag-ray-arb-luh)
I spent the weekend in Paris… and it was lovely.	J'ai passé le week-end à Paris… et c'était très agréable. (zhay pass-ay luh weekend a pa-ree… ay set-ay trez ag-ray-arb-luh)
obligation	obligation (ob-lig-ass-yon)
negotiation	négociation (nay-gos-ee-ass-yon)
determination	détermination (day-term-in-ass-yon)
invited	invité (earn-vit-ay)
prepared	préparé (pray-par-ay)
reserved / booked	réservé (ray-zurv-ay)
ordered	commandé (comm-on-day)
paid	payé (pay-ay)
done	fait (fay)
the bill	l'addition (la-dis-yon)
the dinner	le dîner (luh din-ay)
the roast beef	le rosbif (luh ros-beef)
a table	une table (oon tarb-luh)
a room	une chambre (oon shom-bruh)
a taxi	un taxi (urn taxi)
I have prepared the dinner / I prepared the dinner / I did prepare the dinner.	J'ai préparé le dîner. (zhay pray-par-ay luh din-ay)

I have ordered roast beef for dinner / I ordered roast beef for dinner / I did order roast beef for dinner.	J'ai commandé le rosbif pour le dîner. (zhay comm-on-day luh ros-beef poor luh din-ay)
I have booked a table for you / I booked a table for you / I did book a table for you.	J'ai réservé une table pour vous. (zhay ray-zurv-ay oon tarb-luh poor voo)
She has	Elle a (ell a)
She has booked / reserved a table for this evening – She booked / reserved a table for this evening – She did book / reserve a table for this evening.	Elle a réservé une table pour ce soir. (ell a ray-zurv-ay oon tarb-luh poor sir swar)
He has	Il a (eel a)
He has booked / reserved a room for two people – He booked / reserved a room for two people – He did book / reserve a room for two people.	Il a réservé une chambre pour deux personnes. (eel a ray-zurv-ay oon shom-bruh poor duh purse-on)
We have booked a taxi for you / We booked a taxi for you / We did book a taxi for you.	Nous avons réservé un taxi pour vous. (noo za-von ray-zur-vay urn taxi poor voo)
We paid the bill / We have paid the the bill / We did pay the bill.	Nous avons payé l'addition. (noo za-von pay-ay la-dis-yon)
What? / What is it that?	Qu'est-ce que ? (kess-kuh)
What have you prepared? / What did you prepare?	Qu'est-ce que vous avez préparé ? (kess-kuh voo za-vay pray-par-ay)
What have you done? / What did you do?	Qu'est-ce que vous avez fait ? (kess-kuh voo za-vay fay)
I booked a table, ordered dinner and then paid the bill. What did you do?	J'ai réservé une table, commandé le dîner et puis payé l'addition. Qu'est-ce que vous avez fait ? (zhay ray-zurv-ay oon tarb-luh, comm-on-day luh din-ay ay pwee pay-ay la-dis-yon. kess-kuh voo za-vay fay)
I'm planning to…	J'ai l'intention de… (zhay lon-ton-syon duh)

I'm planning to go back to France in May.	J'ai l'intention de retourner en France en mai. (zhay lon-ton-syon duh ruh-toor-nay on fronce on mey)
I'm scared of...	J'ai peur de... (zhay purr duh)
I'm scared of going back to France in September.	J'ai peur de retourner en France en septembre. (zhay purr duh ruh-toor-nay on fronce on sep-tom-bruh)
Really?	Vraiment ? (vray-mon)
so (therefore)	alors (a-law)
but	mais (may)
I feel like... / I fancy...	J'ai envie de... (zhay on-vee duh)
Yes, I feel like going back to Paris but I'm scared of flying, so I'm planning to take the Eurostar.	Oui, j'ai envie de retourner à Paris mais j'ai peur de l'avion, alors j'ai l'intention de prendre l'Eurostar. (wee zhay on-vee duh ruh-toor-nay a pa-ree may zhay purr duh lav-ee-on, a-law zhay lon-ton-syon duh pron-druh luh-roe-star)
I feel like / fancy buying something this morning.	J'ai envie d'acheter quelque chose ce matin. (zhay on-vee dash-tay kel-kuh shows sir mat-an)
He feels like / fancies reading something this afternoon.	Il a envie de lire quelque chose cet après-midi. (eel a on-vee duh leer kel-kuh shows set ap-ray mi-dee)
They have	Ils ont (eel zon)
They feel like eating something this evening.	Ils ont envie de manger quelque chose ce soir. (eel zon on-vee duh mon-zhay kel-kuh shows sir swar)
I need...	J'ai besoin de... (zhay burz-won duh)
I need to speak French.	J'ai besoin de parler français. (zhay burz-won duh par-lay fron-say)
I need a taxi.	J'ai besoin d'un taxi. (zhay burz-won durn taxi)
I need a room.	J'ai besoin d'une chambre. (zhay burz-won doon shom-bruh)

I need help.	J'ai besoin d'aide. (zhay burz-won daid)
You need help, mate!	Tu as besoin d'aide, mon pote ! (tü a burz-won daid mon pote)
I can't stand… / I hate…	J'ai horreur de… (zhay o-rurr duh)
I can't stand flying! / I can't stand planes! / I hate flying!	J'ai horreur de l'avion ! (zhay o-rurr duh lav-ee-on)
I can't stand eating with my in-laws / I hate eating with my in-laws.	J'ai horreur de manger avec mes beaux-parents. (zhay o-rurr duh mon-zhay av-eck may boe pa-ron)
We can't stand eating with my parents / We hate eating with my parents.	Nous avons horreur de manger avec mes parents. (noo za-von o-rurr duh mon-zhay av-eck may pa-ron)
She can't stand working here / She hates working here.	Elle a horreur de travailler ici. (ell a o-rurr duh trav-eye-ay ee-see)
I was	J'étais (zhet-ay)
necessary	nécessaire (nay-sess-air)
secretary	secrétaire (sek-ray-taire)
salary	salaire (sal air)
I was ordinary.	J'étais ordinaire. (zhet-ay or-din-air)
I was about to… / I was just about to…	J'étais sur le point de… (zhet-ay soor luh pwan duh)
I was about to prepare the dinner / I was just about to prepare the dinner.	J'étais sur le point de préparer le dîner. (zhet-ay soor luh pwan duh pray-par-ay luh din-ay)
I was about to pay the bill.	J'étais sur le point de payer l'addition. (zhet-ay soor luh pwan duh pay-ay la-dis-yon)
I was just about to book a table.	J'étais sur le point de réserver une table. (zhet-ay soor luh pwan duh ray-zurv-ay oon tarb-luh)
You called me / You did call me / You have called me. (formal)	Vous m'avez appelé. (voo ma-vay a-play)
You called me / You did call me / You have called me. (informal)	Tu m'as appelé. (tü ma a-play)
when	quand (kon)

I was just about to book a taxi when you called me.	J'étais sur le point de réserver un taxi quand tu m'as appelé. (zhet-ay soor luh pwan duh ray-zurv-ay urn taxi kon tü ma a-play)
I was about to leave when the telephone rang.	J'étais sur le point de partir quand le téléphone a sonné. (zhet-ay soor luh pwan duh part-ear kon luh tay-lay-fon a sonn-ay)
I was just about to phone you when you knocked at the door. (informal)	J'étais sur le point de te téléphoner quand tu as frappé à la porte. (zhet-ay soor luh pwan duh tuh tay-lay-fone-ay kon tü a frap-ay a la port)
I was just about to order a taxi when it started to rain.	J'étais sur le point de commander un taxi quand il a commencé à pleuvoir. (zhet-ay soor luh pwan duh comm-on-day urn taxi kon deel a com-on-say a pluh-vwar)
so (extremely, very)	tellement (tel-mon)
I am	je suis (zhuh swee)
arrived	arrivé / arrivée (a-reev-ay)
I have arrived / I arrived / I did arrive. (said by a man / boy)	Je suis arrivé. (zhuh swee a-reev-ay)
I have arrived / I arrived / I did arrive. (said by a woman / girl)	Je suis arrivée. (zhuh swee a-reev-ay)
gone	allé / allée (al-ay)
I have gone / I went / I did go. (said by a man / boy)	Je suis allé. (zhuh swee zal-ay)
I have gone / I went / I did go. (said by a woman / girl)	Je suis allée. (zhuh swee zal-ay)
You are (formal)	Vous êtes (voo zet)
You have gone / You went / You did go. (said to a man / boy) – formal	Vous êtes allé. (voo zet al-ay)
You have gone / You went / You did go. (said to a woman / girl) – formal	Vous êtes allée. (voo zet al-ay)

You have arrived / You arrived / You did arrive. (said to a man / boy) – formal	Vous êtes arrivé. (voo zet a-reev-ay)
You have arrived / You arrived / You did arrive. (said to a woman / girl) – formal	Vous êtes arrivée. (voo zet a-reev-ay)
You are (informal)	Tu es (tü ay)
You have arrived / You arrived / You did arrive. (said to a man / boy) – informal	Tu es arrivé. (tü ay a-reev-ay)
You have arrived / You arrived / You did arrive. (said to a woman / girl) – informal	Tu es arrivée. (tü ay a-reev-ay)
I'm sorry.	Je suis désolé / désolée. (zhuh swee dez-oh-lay)
a little / a bit	un peu (urn puh)
I was a little preoccupied / distracted.	J'étais un peu préoccupé / préoccupée. (zhet-ay urn peu pray-ok-oo-pay)
I was in the middle of… (literally "I was in train of…")	J'étais en train de… (zhet-ay on tran duh)
I'm sorry, I was in the middle of eating when you arrived. (informal)	Je suis désolé / désolée, j'étais en train de manger quand tu es arrivé / arrivée. (zhuh swee dez-oh-lay, zhet-ay on tran duh mon-zhay kon tü ay a-reev-ay)
I'm sorry, I was in the middle of preparing dinner when you arrived so I was a bit distracted. (informal)	Je suis désolé / désolée, j'étais en train de préparer le dîner quand tu es arrivé / arrivée, alors j'étais un peu préoccupé / préoccupée. (zhuh swee dez-oh-lay, zhet-ay on tran duh pray-par-ay luh din-ay kon tü ay a-reev-ay a-law zhet-ay urn peu pray-ok-oo-pay)
I was in the middle of writing to you when my mother arrived. (informal)	J'étais en train de t'écrire quand ma mère est arrivée. (zhet-ay on tran duh tay kreer kon ma maire ay ta-reev-ay)

I was in the middle of leaving the house when you phoned me. (informal)	J'étais en train de partir de la maison quand tu m'as téléphoné. (zhet-ay on tran duh part-ear duh la may-zon kon tü ma tay-lay-fone-ay)
I was in the middle of calling you when your letter arrived. (informal)	J'étais en train de t'appeler quand ta lettre est arrivée. (zhet-ay on tran duh tap-lay kon ta let-ruh ay ta-reev-ay)

Wow, Chapter 6 all finished! With each chapter completed, the knowledge you have already gained becomes more secure and your horizons are gradually widened. Have a good break before the next one!

You may well be aware that, in French, words can be masculine or feminine – male or female, if you like. This seems odd to most English speakers, as we don't make this sort of distinction in English. And remembering whether a particular French word is masculine or feminine can seem quite daunting at first.

"How do I know what gender a word is?" people often ask. "How can I possibly learn all of them?" Well, fortunately, the truth is that you don't have to!

For many thousands of words, you can know whether they are masculine or feminine based simply upon what letters those words end in. This means that, by knowing the gender of just a handful of word endings, you will almost instantly know the gender of many thousands of words in French with very little effort or time.

Read through the eight examples below. Once you've done that, try covering up the blue answers in the quiz that follows and see if you can remember which word endings are masculine and which are feminine. But remember, don't try to memorise any of this, instead just read through the list below and then go through the quiz as many times as you need to until you begin to get a feel for which words take which gender.

Masculine	Feminine
Words ending "ard" are normally masculine. Some examples: "standard", "blizzard", "lézard" (lizard) – masculine, masculine, masculine.	**Words ending "ion" are normally feminine.** Some examples: "information", "question", "éducation" – feminine, feminine, feminine.
Words ending "age" are normally masculine. Some examples: "passage", "bandage", "courage" – masculine, masculine, masculine.	**Words ending "ure" are normally feminine.** Some examples: "nature", "structure", "culture" – feminine, feminine, feminine.

Masculine	Feminine
Words ending "eau" are normally masculine. Some examples: "plateau", "bureau", "gâteau" – masculine, masculine, masculine.	**Words ending "ude" are normally feminine.** Some examples: "attitude", "gratitude", "solitude" – feminine, feminine, feminine.
Words ending in "isme" are normally masculine. Some examples: "socialisme", "racisme", "optimisme" – masculine, masculine, masculine.	**Words ending "ance" are normally feminine.** Some examples: "chance", "importance", "alliance" – feminine, feminine, feminine.
Words ending in "ment" are normally masculine. Some examples: "mouvement" (movement), "gouvernement" (government), "moment" – masculine, masculine, masculine.	**Words ending "té" are normally feminine.** Some examples: "université" (university), "qualité" (quality), "activité" (activity) – feminine, feminine, feminine.

Masculine or feminine – Quiz time

For this simple quiz, all you need to do (as per usual) is to cover up the blue and see if you can work out the gender (given below each word) based on the word endings, as shown above. You'll find you get better as you progress through the words.

Once you have gone through them, feel free to do it all over again – because remember, you're not simply learning the gender of the words here, you're learning the gender of the many thousands of words that all share these endings.

Keep at this until you can get most of them correct, after which I suggest that you wait a few days and then come back and try again. Having a break and then coming back to revisit something can really help you to store things in your long-term memory.

Okay now, off you go!

blizzard	**gouvernement**	**attitude**	**optimisme**
masculine	masculine	feminine	masculine
structure	**chance**	**plateau**	**lézard**
feminine	feminine	masculine	masculine
moment	**alliance**	**courage**	**gratitude**
masculine	feminine	masculine	feminine
bureau	**qualité**	**racisme**	**information**
masculine	feminine	masculine	feminine
bandage	**nature**	**attitude**	**question**
masculine	feminine	feminine	feminine

CHAPTER 7

I'm moving to France in July
because of you!
BECAUSE of me?
You mean *THANKS* to me!

> I'm moving to France in July because of you!
> BECAUSE of me? You mean THANKS to me!

You help someone change their life and this is the thanks you get!

Well, you may already know how to be ungrateful in English, so let me teach you how to be ungrateful in French!

What is "in May" in French?

en mai
(on mey)

And "in September"?

en septembre
(on sep-tom-bruh)

"July" in French is:

juillet
(zhoo-ee-ay)

So how would you say "in July"?

en juillet
(on zhoo-ee-ay)

And again, how would you say "I visited"?

J'ai visité.
(zhay visit-ay)

And what about "I visited Paris"?

J'ai visité Paris.
(zhay visit-ay pa-ree)

So, how would you say "I visited Paris in July"?

J'ai visité Paris en juillet.
(zhay visit-ay pa-ree on zhoo-ee-ay)

What is "I'm planning to..."?

J'ai l'intention de...
(zhay lon-ton-syon duh)

"Visit" or "to visit" in French is:

visiter
(visit-ay)[10]

Okay, how would you say "I'm planning to visit..."?

J'ai l'intention de visiter...
(zhay lon-ton-syon duh visit-ay)

---

10 In case you're wondering, yes, "to visit" (visiter) does sound exactly the same as "visited" (visité) in French but don't worry because the context will always make it clear which is being used.

And how would you say "I'm planning to visit Paris in July"?

J'ai l'intention de visiter Paris en juillet.
(zhay lon-ton-syon duh visit-ay pa-ree on zhoo-ee-ay)

What is "to go back" or "to return" in French?

retourner
(ruh-toor-nay)

So, how would you say "I'm planning to go back"?

J'ai l'intention de retourner
(zhay lon-ton-syon duh ruh-toor-nay)

And what is "in France" or "to France"?

en France
(on fronce)

Alright, how would you say "I'm planning to go back to France in July"?

J'ai l'intention de retourner en France en juillet.
(zhay lon-ton-syon duh ruh-toor-nay on fronce on zhoo-ee-ay)

"I'm moving" in French is:

Je déménage
(zhuh day-may-nazh)

It's always useful, when learning a foreign language, to understand what each of the bits in the sentence actually mean.

"I'm moving" in French is a good example of this – of how knowing what each word actually means can make the words both more memorable and understandable.

In this example, the "je" means "I" and "déménage" can actually be broken into two bits.

The "ménage" part is a word English speakers tend to be familiar with from the phrase "ménage à trois", which means (among other things!) a "household of three" – "ménage" meaning "household".

The "dé" bit of "déménage", on the other hand, means "dis" – like the "dis" in "disappear" or "dislike".

So, "déménage" should start to seem like a fairly logical way to say you are moving house since it literally means to "dis-household" yourself. After all, when you move, you do sort of dis-household yourself in one place and then re-household yourself in another. Well, it makes sense to me anyway.

Still, as I say, it is always worth trying to see if you can break a strange or unfamiliar word into bits like this, because when you really understand where a word has come from, you tend to remember it and comprehend it far more easily.

So, again, "I'm moving" in French is literally "I'm dis-householding", which is:

Je déménage
(zhuh day-may-nazh)

Now, how would you say "to France"?

en France
(on fronce)

And again, what is "I'm moving" (literally "I'm dis-householding")?

Je déménage
(zhuh day-may-nazh)

So, how would you say "I'm moving to France"?

Je déménage en France.
(zhuh day-may-nazh on fronce)

How about "I'm moving to France in July?"

Je déménage en France en juillet.
(zhuh day-may-nazh on fronce on zhoo-ee-ay)

What about "I'm moving to France in September"?

Je déménage en France en septembre.
(zhuh day-may-nazh on fronce on sep-tom-bruh)

And how would you say "in Paris" or "to Paris"?

à Paris
(a pa-ree)

How would you say "I'm moving to Paris in September"?

Je déménage à Paris en septembre.
(zhuh day-may-nazh a pa-ree on sep-tom-bruh)

What is "you have" (formal) in French?

Vous avez
(voo za-vay)

Which of those words means "you"?

Vous
(voo)

"Because of…" in French is:

à cause de…
(a koze duh)

Literally this means "at cause of…"
So, how would you say "because of you" (formal) – literally "at cause of you"?

à cause de vous
(a koze duh voo)

Let's try saying "I'm moving to Paris in September because of you!" (formal)
(literally "I dis-household to Paris in September at cause of you!")

Je déménage à Paris en septembre à cause de vous !
(zhuh day-may-nazh a pa-ree on sep-tom-bruh a koze duh voo)

Now try "I'm moving to Paris in July because of you!" (formal)

Je déménage à Paris en juillet à cause de vous !
(zhuh day-may-nazh a pa-ree on zhoo-ee-ay a koze duh voo)

What is "to France"?

en France
(on fronce)

How would you say "I'm moving to France in July because of you!" (formal)?

Je déménage en France en juillet à cause de vous !
(zhuh day-may-nazh on fronce on zhoo-ee-ay a koze duh voo)

"Because of you" (informal) in French is:

à cause de toi
(a koze duh twah)

So, how would you say "I'm moving to France in July because of you!" (informal)?

Je déménage en France en juillet à cause de toi !
(zhuh day-may-nazh on fronce on zhoo-ee-ay a koze duh twah)

How about "I'm moving to Paris in July because of you!" (informal)?

Je déménage à Paris en juillet à cause de toi !
(zhuh day-may-nazh a pa-ree on zhoo-ee-ay a koze duh twah)

"Because of me" in French is:

à cause de moi
(a koze duh mwah)

Why not turn this into a question by raising your voice at the end and ask "because of me?"?

À cause de moi ?
(a koze duh mwah)

So, you have now learnt how to say "because of" in French. It is a very useful phrase which can be used both in a fairly neutral way or, if you want, in a very negative way to attribute blame: "I lost my money because of you!" or "I never got married because of you!" Heady stuff, yes!

"Because of" actually has a partner that has a similar meaning except that it is more positive and means "thanks to…".
You will want to use this phrase for nice things, such as
"Thanks to you, I found my money in the end" or
"Thanks to you, I met and married a wonderful person!".

"Thanks to..." in French is literally "grace to...", which is:

grâce à...
(gras a)

So, how would you say "thanks to you!" (informal)?

Grâce à toi !
(gras a twah)

How about "thanks to you!" (formal)?

Grâce à vous !
(gras a voo)

And how would you say "thanks to me!"?

Grâce à moi !
(gras a mwah)

"Do you want...?" in French is literally "want you?", which, when speaking formally, is:

Voulez-vous...?
(voo-lay voo)

How would you say "do you want to prepare the dinner?" (formal) – (literally "want you to prepare the dinner?")?

Voulez-vous préparer le dîner ?
(voo-lay voo pray-par-ay luh din-ay)

What is "this evening" in French?

ce soir
(sir swar)

So, how would you say "do you want to prepare the dinner this evening?" (formal) – (literally "want you to prepare the dinner this evening?")?

Voulez-vous préparer le dîner ce soir ?
(voo-lay voo pray-par-ay luh din-ay sir swar)

What is "to eat something"?

manger quelque chose
(mon-zhay kel-kuh shows)

How would you now say "do you want to eat something?" (formal)?

Voulez-vous manger quelque chose ?
(voo-lay voo mon-zhay kel-kuh shows)

How about "do you want to buy something?" (formal)?

Voulez-vous acheter quelque chose ?
(voo-lay voo ash-tay kel-kuh shows)

What is "to pay the bill"?

payer l'addition
(pay-ay la-dis-yon)

So, how would you say "do you want to pay the bill?" (formal)?

Voulez-vous payer l'addition ?
(voo-lay voo pay-ay la-dis-yon)

How about "do you want to book a taxi?" (formal)?

Voulez-vous réserver un taxi ?
(voo-lay voo ray-zur-vay urn taxi)

"Do you want to go back to France in July?" (formal)

Voulez-vous retourner en France en juillet ?
(voo-lay voo ruh-toor-nay on fronce on zhoo-ee-ay)

You know that "do you want?" is literally "want you?", which is "voulez-vous?".
Let's turn these words the other way around now and simply say "you want"
(formal), which will be:

Vous voulez
(voo voo-lay)

So, how would you say as a statement "you want to go back to France in July!" (formal)?

Vous voulez retourner en France en juillet !
(*voo voo-lay ruh-toor-nay on fronce on zhoo-ee-ay*)

And how about "you want to go back to Paris in July!" (formal)

Vous voulez retourner à Paris en juillet !
(*voo voo-lay ruh-toor-nay a pa-ree on zhoo-ee-ay*)

And how would you say "you want to pay the bill!" (formal)?

Vous voulez payer l'addition !
(*voo voo-lay pay-ay la-dis-yon*)

"To say" in French is:

dire
(*dear*)

How would you say "you want to say" (formal)?

Vous voulez dire
(*voo voolay dear*)

Interestingly, "you want to say" is actually the way that French speakers say "you mean". So if, for example, a French person wants to say "what do you mean?" then they will ask "what do you want to say?".

So, to begin with, how would you say "you mean" in French (formal) – (literally "you want to say")?

Vous voulez dire
(*voo voolay dear*)

And again what is "thanks to"?

Grâce à…
(*gras a*)

And "thanks to me"?

Grâce à moi.
(*gras a mwah*)

And once more, how would you say "you mean" (formal) – (literally "you want to say")?

Vous voulez dire
(*voo voolay dear*)

How would you say "you mean *thanks* to me!" (formal)?

Vous voulez dire *grâce* à moi !
(*voo voolay dear gras a mwah*)

Right, let's go back to our initial dialogue. To begin with, how would someone say "I'm moving to France" (literally "I'm dis-householding to France")?

Je déménage en France.
(*zhuh day-may-nazh on fronce*)

And how would you say "in July"?

en juillet
(*on zhoo-ee-ay*)

And again how would you say "because of you" (informal) – (literally "at cause of you")?

à cause de toi !
(*a koze duh twah*)

Putting this all together, how would you say "I'm moving to France in July because of you" (informal)?

Je déménage en France en juillet à cause de toi !
(*zhuh day-may-nazh on fronce on zhoo-ee-ay a koze duh twah*)

And how would you say "because of you" (formal)?

à cause de vous !
(*a koze duh voo*)

So, how would you say "I'm moving to France in July because of you" (formal)?

Je déménage en France en juillet à cause de vous !
(*zhuh day-may-nazh on fronce on zhoo-ee-ay a koze duh voo*)

And what is "because of me"?

À *cause de* moi ?
(a koze duh mwah)

How would you reply "Because of me? You mean *thanks* to me!" (formal) (literally "At cause of me? You want to say grace to me!")?

À *cause de* moi ? Vous voulez dire *grâce* à moi !
(a koze duh mwah voo voolay dear gras a mwah)

Now try the entire dialogue below and see how you get on. Take your time and think out each step bit by bit until it all comes naturally and effortlessly. And remember, there's no rush!

I'm moving to France in July because of you! (formal)
Je déménage en France en juillet à *cause de* vous !
(zhuh day-may-nazh on fronce on zhoo-ee-ay a koze duh voo)

Because of me? You mean *thanks* to me! (formal)
À *cause de* moi ? Vous voulez dire *grâce* à moi !
(a koze duh mwah voo voolay dear gras a mwah)

Building Blocks 7

Some especially useful building blocks this time, I'm sure you'll agree:

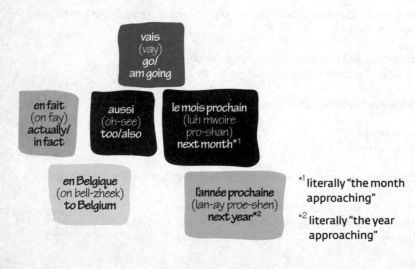

vais
(vay)
go/
am going

en fait
(on fay)
actually/
in fact

aussi
(oh-see)
too/also

le mois prochain
(luh mwoire
pro-shan)
next month[*1]

en Belgique
(on bell-zheek)
to Belgium

l'année prochaine
(lan-ay proe-shen)
next year[*2]

[*1] literally "the month approaching"

[*2] literally "the year approaching"

There are five columns on this occasion. More columns of course equal even more fun!

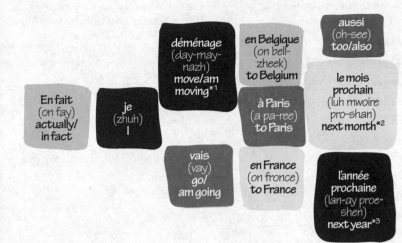

En fait
(on fay)
actually/
in fact

je
(zhuh)
I

déménage
(day-may-nazh)
move/am
moving*1

en Belgique
(on bell-zheek)
to Belgium

aussi
(oh-see)
too/also

le mois
prochain
(luh mwoire
pro-shan)
next month*2

à Paris
(a pa-ree)
to Paris

vais
(vay)
go/
am going

en France
(on fronce)
to France

l'année
prochaine
(lan-ay proe-shen)
next year*3

*1 literally "am dis-householding"

*2 literally "the month approaching"

*3 literally "the year approaching"

Checklist 7

The penultimate checklist – you're almost there...

le week-end (luh weekend)	the weekend
égocentrique (ay-go-son-treek)	egocentric
anémique (an-ay-meek)	anaemic
méthodique (may-toad-eek)	methodical
pratique (prat-eek)	practical
enthousiaste (on-tooze-ee-ast)	enthusiastic
J'ai (zhay)	I have
visité (visit-ay)	visited
J'ai visité (zhay visit-ay)	I have visited / I visited / I did visit
Paris (pa-ree)	Paris

Notre-Dame (not-re darm)	Notre-Dame
J'ai visité Notre-Dame. (zhay visit-ay not-re darm)	I have visited Notre-Dame / I visited Notre-Dame / I did visit Notre-Dame.
passé (pass-ay)	spent
J'ai passé (zhay pass-ay)	I have spent / I spent / I did spend
Vous avez (voo za-vay)	You have
Vous avez passé (voo za-vay pass-ay)	You have spent / You spent / You did spend
Nous avons (noo za-von)	We have
Nous avons passé (noo za-von pass-ay)	We have spent / We spent / We did spend
septembre (sep-tom-bruh)	September
Noël (no-ell)	Christmas
à Paris (a pa-ree)	in Paris
en France (on fronce)	in France
en Suisse (on swees)	in Switzerland
Nous avons passé Noël en Suisse. (noo za-von pass-ay no-ell on swees)	We have spent Christmas in Switzerland / We spent Christmas in Switzerland / We did spend Christmas in Switzerland.
Vous avez passé septembre en France. (voo za-vay pass-ay sep-tom-bruh on fronce)	You have spent September in France / You spent September in France / You did spend September in France.
et (ay)	and
c'était (set-ay)	it was
C'était fantastique. (set-ay fon-tass-teek)	It was fantastic.
très agréable (trez ag-ray-arb-luh)	lovely / very agreeable
C'était très agréable. (set-ay trez ag-ray-arb-luh)	It was lovely. / It was very agreeable.
J'ai passé le week-end à Paris… et c'était très agréable. (zhay pass-ay luh weekend a pa-ree… ay set-ay trez ag-ray-arb-luh)	I spent the weekend in Paris… and it was lovely.
million (mil-yon)	million

décision (day-sizz-yon)	decision
attention (at-ons-yon)	attention
invité (earn-vit-ay)	invited
préparé (pray-par-ay)	prepared
réservé (ray-zurv-ay)	reserved / booked
commandé (comm-on-day)	ordered
payé (pay-ay)	paid
fait (fay)	done
l'addition (la-dis-yon)	the bill
le dîner (luh din-ay)	the dinner
le rosbif (luh ros-beef)	the roast beef
une table (oon tarb-luh)	a table
une chambre (oon shom-bruh)	a room
un taxi (urn taxi)	a taxi
J'ai préparé le dîner. (zhay pray-par-ay luh din-ay)	I have prepared the dinner / I prepared the dinner / I did prepare the dinner.
J'ai commandé le rosbif pour le dîner. (zhay comm-on-day luh ros-beef poor luh din-ay)	I have ordered roast beef for dinner / I ordered roast beef for dinner / I did order roast beef for dinner.
J'ai réservé une table pour vous. (zhay ray-zurv-ay oon tarb-luh poor voo)	I have booked a table for you / I booked a table for you / I did book a table for you.
Elle a (ell a)	She has
Elle a réservé une table pour ce soir. (ell a ray-zurv-ay oon tarb-luh poor sir swar)	She has booked / reserved a table for this evening – She booked / reserved a table for this evening – She did book / reserve a table for this evening.
Il a (eel a)	He has
Il a réservé une chambre pour deux personnes. (eel a ray-zurv-ay oon shom-bruh poor duh purse-on)	He has booked / reserved a room for two people – He booked / reserved a room for two people – He did book / reserve a room for two people.

Nous avons réservé un taxi pour vous. (noo za-von ray-zur-vay urn taxi poor voo)	We have booked a taxi for you / We booked a taxi for you / We did book a taxi for you.
Nous avons payé l'addition. (noo za-von pay-ay la-dis-yon)	We paid the bill / We have paid the the bill / We did pay the bill.
Qu'est-ce que ? (kess-kuh)	What? / What is it that?
Qu'est-ce que vous avez préparé ? (kess-kuh voo za-vay pray-par-ay)	What have you prepared? / What did you prepare? (literally "What is it that you have prepared?")
Qu'est-ce que vous avez fait ? (kess-kuh voo za-vay fay)	What have you done? / What did you do? (literally "What is it that you have done?")
J'ai réservé une table, commandé le dîner et puis payé l'addition. Qu'est-ce que vous avez fait ? (zhay ray-zurv-ay oon tarb-luh, comm-on-day luh din-ay ay pwee pay-ay la-dis-yon. kess-kuh voo za-vay fay)	I booked a table, ordered dinner and then paid the bill. What did you do?
J'ai l'intention de… (zhay lon-ton-syon duh)	I'm planning to… (literally "I have the intention of…")
J'ai l'intention de retourner en France en mai. (zhay lon-ton-syon duh ruh-toor-nay on fronce on mey)	I'm planning to go back to France in May.
J'ai peur de… (zhay purr duh)	I'm scared of… (literally "I have fear of…")
J'ai peur de retourner en France en septembre. (zhay purr duh ruh-toor-nay on fronce on sep-tom-bruh)	I'm scared of going back to France in September.
Vraiment ? (vray-mon)	Really?
alors (a-law)	so (therefore)
mais (may)	but
J'ai envie de… (zhay on-vee duh)	I feel like… / I fancy… (literally "I have envy of…")

Oui, j'ai envie de retourner à Paris mais j'ai peur de l'avion, alors j'ai l'intention de prendre l'Eurostar. (wee zhay on-vee duh ruh-toor-nay a pa-ree may zhay purr duh lav-ee-on, a-law zhay lon-ton-syon duh pron-druh luh-roe-star)	Yes, I feel like going back to Paris but I'm scared of flying, so I'm planning to take the Eurostar.
J'ai envie d'acheter quelque chose ce matin. (zhay on-vee dash-tay kel-kuh shows sir mat-an)	I feel like / fancy buying something this morning.
Il a envie de lire quelque chose cet après-midi. (eel a on-vee duh leer kel-kuh shows set ap-ray mi-dee)	He feels like / fancies reading something this afternoon.
Ils ont (eel zon)	They have
Ils ont envie de manger quelque chose ce soir. (eel zon on-vee duh mon-zhay kel-kuh shows sir swar)	They feel like eating something this evening.
J'ai besoin de… (zhay burz-won duh)	I need… (literally "I have need of…")
J'ai besoin de parler français. (zhay burz-won duh par-lay fron-say)	I need to speak French.
J'ai besoin d'un taxi. (zhay burz-won durn taxi)	I need a taxi.
J'ai besoin d'une chambre. (zhay burz-won doon shom-bruh)	I need a room.
J'ai besoin d'aide. (zhay burz-won daid)	I need help.
Tu as besoin d'aide, mon pote ! (tü a burz-won daid mon pote)	You need help, mate!
J'ai horreur de… (zhay o-rurr duh)	I can't stand… / I hate… (literally "I have horror of…")
J'ai horreur de l'avion ! (zhay o-rurr duh lav-ee-on)	I can't stand flying! / I can't stand planes! / I hate flying!
J'ai horreur de manger avec mes beaux-parents. (zhay o-rurr duh mon-zhay av-eck may boe pa-ron)	I can't stand eating with my in-laws / I hate eating with my in-laws.
Nous avons horreur de manger avec mes parents. (noo za-von o-rurr duh mon-zhay av-eck may pa-ron)	We can't stand eating with my parents / We hate eating with my parents.

Elle a horreur de travailler ici. (ell a o-rurr duh trav-eye-ay ee-see)	She can't stand working here / she hates working here.
J'étais (zhet-ay)	I was
dictionnaire (dik-syon-air)	dictionary
révolutionnaire (ray-vol-oos-yon-air)	revolutionary
vocabulaire (voe-kab-you-laire)	vocabulary
J'étais ordinaire. (zhet-ay or-din-air)	I was ordinary.
J'étais sur le point de… (zhet-ay soor luh pwan duh)	I was about to… / I was just about to… (literally "I was on the point of…")
J'étais sur le point de préparer le dîner. (zhet-ay soor luh pwan duh pray-par-ay luh din-ay)	I was about to prepare the dinner / I was just about to prepare the dinner.
J'étais sur le point de payer l'addition. (zhet-ay soor luh pwan duh pay-ay la-dis-yon)	I was about to pay the bill.
J'étais sur le point de réserver une table. (zhet-ay soor luh pwan duh ray-zurv-ay oon tarb-luh)	I was just about to book a table.
Vous m'avez appelé. (voo ma-vay a-play)	You called me / You did call me / You have called me. (formal)
Tu m'as appelé. (tü ma a-play)	You called me / You did call me / You have called me. (informal)
quand (kon)	when
J'étais sur le point de réserver un taxi quand tu m'as appelé. (zhet-ay soor luh pwan duh ray-zurv-ay urn taxi kon tü ma a-play)	I was just about to book a taxi when you called me.
J'étais sur le point de partir quand le téléphone a sonné. (zhet-ay soor luh pwan duh part-ear kon luh tay-lay-fon a sonn-ay)	I was about to leave when the telephone rang.
J'étais sur le point de te téléphoner quand tu as frappé à la porte. (zhet-ay soor luh pwan duh tuh tay-lay-fone-ay kon tü a frap-ay a la port)	I was just about to phone you when you knocked at the door. (informal)

J'étais sur le point de commander un taxi quand il a commencé à pleuvoir. (zhet-ay soor luh pwan duh comm-on-day urn taxi kon deel a com-on-say a pluh-vwar)	I was just about to order a taxi when it started to rain.
tellement (tel-mon)	so (extremely, very)
je suis (zhuh swee)	I am
arrivé / arrivée (a-reev-ay)	arrived
Je suis arrivé. (zhuh swee a-reev-ay)	I have arrived / I arrived / I did arrive. (said by a man / boy)
Je suis arrivée. (zhuh swee a-reev-ay)	I have arrived / I arrived / I did arrive. (said by a woman / girl)
allé / allée (al-ay)	gone
Je suis allé. (zhuh swee zal-ay)	I have gone / I went / I did go. (said by a man / boy)
Je suis allée. (zhuh swee zal-ay)	I have gone / I went / I did go. (said by a woman / girl)
Vous êtes (voo zet)	You are (formal)
Vous êtes allé. (voo zet al-ay)	You have gone / You went / You did go. (said to a man / boy) – formal
Vous êtes allée. (voo zet al-ay)	You have gone / You went / You did go. (said to a woman / girl) – formal
Vous êtes arrivé. (voo zet a-reev-ay)	You have arrived / You arrived / You did arrive. (said to a man / boy) – formal
Vous êtes arrivée. (voo zet a-reev-ay)	You have arrived / You arrived / You did arrive. (said to a woman / girl) – formal
Tu es (tü ay)	You are (informal)
Tu es arrivé. (tü ay a-reev-ay)	You have arrived / You arrived / You did arrive. (said to a man / boy) – informal
Tu es arrivée. (tü ay a-reev-ay)	You have arrived / You arrived / You did arrive. (said to a woman / girl) – informal

Je suis désolé / désolée. (zhuh swee dez-oh-lay)	I'm sorry.
un peu (urn puh)	a little / a bit
J'étais un peu préoccupé / préoccupée. (zhet-ay urn puh pray-ok-oo-pay)	I was a little preoccupied / distracted.
J'étais en train de... (zhet-ay on tran duh)	I was in the middle of... (literally "I was in train of...")
Je suis désolé / désolée, j'étais en train de manger quand tu es arrivé / arrivée. (zhuh swee dez-oh-lay, zhet-ay on tran duh mon-zhay kon tü ay a-reev-ay)	I'm sorry, I was in the middle of eating when you arrived. (informal)
Je suis désolé / désolée, j'étais en train de préparer le dîner quand tu es arrivé / arrivée, alors j'étais un peu préoccupé / préoccupée. (zhuh swee dez-oh-lay, zhet-ay on tran duh pray-par-ay luh din-ay kon tü ay a-reev-ay a-law zhet-ay urn puh pray-ok-oo-pay)	I'm sorry, I was in the middle of preparing dinner when you arrived so I was a bit distracted. (informal)
J'étais en train de t'écrire quand ma mère est arrivée. (zhet-ay on tran duh tay kreer kon ma maire ay ta-reev-ay)	I was in the middle of writing to you when my mother arrived. (informal)
J'étais en train de partir de la maison quand tu m'as téléphoné. (zhet-ay on tran duh part-ear duh la may-zon kon tü ma tay-lay-fone-ay)	I was in the middle of leaving the house when you phoned me. (informal)
J'étais en train de t'appeler quand ta lettre est arrivée. (zhet-ay on tran duh tap-lay kon ta let-ruh ay ta-reev-ay)	I was in the middle of calling you when your letter arrived. (informal)
juillet (zhoo-ee-ay)	July
en juillet (on zhoo-ee-ay)	in July
J'ai visité Paris en juillet. (zhay visit-ay pa-ree on zhoo-ee-ay)	I visited Paris in July / I have visited Paris in July / I did visit Paris in July.

J'ai l'intention de visiter Paris en juillet. (zhay lon-ton-syon duh visit-ay pa-ree on zhoo-ee-ay)	I'm planning to visit Paris in July.
Je déménage (zhuh day-may-nazh)	I'm moving (literally "I dis-household" / "I'm dis-householding")
Je déménage en France en septembre. (zhuh day-may-nazh on fronce on sep-tom-bruh)	I'm moving to France in September.
à cause de... (a koze duh)	because of (literally "at cause of")
à cause de vous (a koze duh voo)	because of you (formal)
à cause de toi (a koze duh twah)	because of you (informal)
grâce à... (gras a)	thanks to (literally "grace to")
Grâce à moi ! (gras a mwah)	Thanks to me!
Grâce à vous ! (gras a voo)	Thanks to you! (formal)
Grâce à toi ! (gras a twah)	Thanks to you! (informal)
Je déménage en France en juillet à cause de toi ! (zhuh day-may-nazh on fronce on zhoo-ee-ay a koze duh twah)	I'm moving to France in July because of you! (informal)
Voulez-vous ? (voo-lay voo)	Do you want? (literally "want you?") – (formal)
Voulez-vous préparer le dîner ce soir ? (voo-lay voo pray-par-ay luh din-ay sir swar)	Do you want to prepare the dinner this evening? (formal)
Voulez-vous manger quelque chose ? (voo-lay voo mon-zhay kel-kuh shows)	Do you want to eat something? (formal)
Vous voulez (voo voo-lay)	You want (formal)
dire (dear)	to say
Vous voulez dire (voo voolay dear)	You mean (literally "you want to say") – (formal)
Je déménage en France en juillet à cause de vous ! (zhuh day-may-nazh on fronce on zhoo-ee-ay a koze duh voo)	I'm moving to France in July because of you! (formal)
À cause de moi ? Vous voulez dire grâce à moi ! (a koze duh mwah voo voolay dear gras a mwah)	Because of me? You mean *thanks* to me! (formal)

En fait, je déménage en Belgique aussi. (on fay, zhuh day-may-nazh on bell-zheek oh-see)	Actually, I'm moving to Belgium too.
En fait, je déménage en France le mois prochain. (on fay, zhuh day-may-nazh on fronce luh mwoire pro-shan)	Actually, I'm moving to France next month.
En fait, je vais à Paris l'année prochaine. (on fay, zhuh vay a pa-ree lan-ay proe-shen)	Actually, I'm going to Paris next year.

Flip-flop time!

the weekend	**le week-end** (luh weekend)
egocentric	**égocentrique** (ay-go-son-treek)
anaemic	**anémique** (an-ay-meek)
methodical	**méthodique** (may-toad-eek)
practical	**pratique** (prat-eek)
enthusiastic	**enthousiaste** (on-tooze-ee-ast)
I have	**J'ai** (zhay)
visited	**visité** (visit-ay)
I have visited / I visited / I did visit	**J'ai visité** (zhay visit-ay)
Paris	**Paris** (pa-ree)
Notre-Dame	**Notre-Dame** (not-re darm)
I have visited Notre-Dame / I visited Notre-Dame / I did visit Notre-Dame.	**J'ai visité Notre-Dame.** (zhay visit-ay not-re darm)
spent	**passé** (pass-ay)
I have spent / I spent / I did spend	**J'ai passé** (zhay pass-ay)
You have (formal)	**Vous avez** (voo za-vay)
You have spent / You spent / You did spend (formal)	**Vous avez passé** (voo za-vay pass-ay)
We have	**Nous avons** (noo za-von)

We have spent / We spent / We did spend	Nous avons passé (noo za-von pass-ay)
September	septembre (sep-tom-bruh)
Christmas	Noël (no-ell)
in Paris	à Paris (a pa-ree)
in France	en France (on fronce)
in Switzerland	en Suisse (on Swees)
We have spent Christmas in Switzerland / We spent Christmas in Switzerland / We did spend Christmas in Switzerland.	Nous avons passé Noël en Suisse. (noo za-von pass-ay no-ell on swees)
You have spent September in France / You spent September in France / You did spend September in France. (formal)	Vous avez passé septembre en France. (voo za-vay pass-ay sep-tom-bruh on fronce)
and	et (ay)
it was	c'était (set-ay)
It was fantastic.	C'était fantastique. (set-ay fon-tass-teek)
lovely / very agreeable	très agréable (trez ag-ray-arb-luh)
It was lovely. / It was very agreeable.	C'était très agréable. (set-ay trez ag-ray-arb-luh)
I spent the weekend in Paris… and it was lovely.	J'ai passé le week-end à Paris… et c'était très agréable. (zhay pass-ay luh weekend a pa-ree… ay set-ay trez ag-ray-arb-luh)
million	million (mil-yon)
decision	décision (day-sizz-yon)
attention	attention (at-ons-yon)
invited	invité (earn-vit-ay)
prepared	préparé (pray-par-ay)
reserved / booked	réservé (ray-zurv-ay)
ordered	commandé (comm-on-day)
paid	payé (pay-ay)

done	fait (fay)
the bill	l'addition (la-dis-yon)
the dinner	le dîner (luh din-ay)
the roast beef	le rosbif (luh ros-beef)
a table	une table (oon tarb-luh)
a room	une chambre (oon shom-bruh)
a taxi	un taxi (urn taxi)
I have prepared the dinner / I prepared the dinner / I did prepare the dinner.	J'ai préparé le dîner. (zhay pray-par-ay luh din-ay)
I have ordered roast beef for dinner / I ordered roast beef for dinner / I did order roast beef for dinner.	J'ai commandé le rosbif pour le dîner. (zhay comm-on-day luh ros-beef poor luh din-ay)
I have booked a table for you / I booked a table for you / I did book a table for you.	J'ai réservé une table pour vous. (zhay ray-zurv-ay oon tarb-luh poor voo)
She has	Elle a (ell a)
She has booked / reserved a table for this evening – She booked / reserved a table for this evening – She did book / reserve a table for this evening.	Elle a réservé une table pour ce soir. (ell a ray-zurv-ay oon tarb-luh poor sir swar)
He has	Il a (eel a)
He has booked / reserved a room for two people – He booked / reserved a room for two people – He did book / reserve a room for two people.	Il a réservé une chambre pour deux personnes. (eel a ray-zurv-ay oon shom-bruh poor duh purse-on)
We have booked a taxi for you / We booked a taxi for you / We did book a taxi for you.	Nous avons réservé un taxi pour vous. (noo za-von ray-zur-vay urn taxi poor voo)
We paid the bill / We have paid the the bill / We did pay the bill.	Nous avons payé l'addition. (noo za-von pay-ay la-dis-yon)
What? / What is it that?	Qu'est-ce que ? (kess-kuh)
What have you prepared? / What did you prepare?	Qu'est-ce que vous avez préparé ? (kess-kuh voo za-vay pray-par-ay)

What have you done? / What did you do?	Qu'est-ce que vous avez fait ? (kess-kuh voo za-vay fay)
I booked a table, ordered dinner and then paid the bill. What did you do?	J'ai réservé une table, commandé le dîner et puis payé l'addition. Qu'est-ce que vous avez fait ? (zhay ray-zurv-ay oon tarb-luh, comm-on-day luh din-ay ay pwee pay-ay la-dis-yon. kess-kuh voo za-vay fay)
I'm planning to…	J'ai l'intention de… (zhay lon-ton-syon duh)
I'm planning to go back to France in May.	J'ai l'intention de retourner en France en mai. (zhay lon-ton-syon duh ruh-toor-nay on fronce on mey)
I'm scared of…	J'ai peur de… (zhay purr duh)
I'm scared of going back to France in September.	J'ai peur de retourner en France en septembre. (zhay purr duh ruh-toor-nay on fronce on sep-tom-bruh)
Really?	Vraiment ? (vray-mon)
so (therefore)	alors (a-law)
but	mais (may)
I feel like… / I fancy…	J'ai envie de… (zhay on-vee duh)
Yes, I feel like going back to Paris but I'm scared of flying, so I'm planning to take the Eurostar.	Oui, j'ai envie de retourner à Paris mais j'ai peur de l'avion, alors j'ai l'intention de prendre l'Eurostar. (wee zhay on-vee duh ruh-toor-nay a pa-ree may zhay purr duh lav-ee-on, a-law zhay lon-ton-syon duh pron-druh luh-roe-star)
I feel like / fancy buying something this morning.	J'ai envie d'acheter quelque chose ce matin. (zhay on-vee dash-tay kel-kuh shows sir mat-an)
He feels like / fancies reading something this afternoon.	Il a envie de lire quelque chose cet après-midi. (eel a on-vee duh leer kel-kuh shows set ap-ray mi-dee)
They have	Ils ont (eel zon)

They feel like eating something this evening.	Ils ont envie de manger quelque chose ce soir. (eel zon on-vee duh mon-zhay kel-kuh shows sir swar)
I need...	J'ai besoin de... (zhay burz-won duh)
I need to speak French.	J'ai besoin de parler français. (zhay burz-won duh par-lay fron-say)
I need a taxi.	J'ai besoin d'un taxi. (zhay burz-won durn taxi)
I need a room.	J'ai besoin d'une chambre. (zhay burz-won doon shom-bruh)
I need help.	J'ai besoin d'aide. (zhay burz-won daid)
You need help, mate!	Tu as besoin d'aide, mon pote ! (tü a burz-won daid mon pote)
I can't stand... / I hate...	J'ai horreur de... (zhay o-rurr duh)
I can't stand flying! / I can't stand planes! / I hate flying!	J'ai horreur de l'avion ! (zhay o-rurr duh lav-ee-on)
I can't stand eating with my in-laws / I hate eating with my in-laws.	J'ai horreur de manger avec mes beaux-parents. (zhay o-rurr duh mon-zhay av-eck may boe pa-ron)
We can't stand eating with my parents / We hate eating with my parents.	Nous avons horreur de manger avec mes parents. (noo za-von o-rurr duh mon-zhay av-eck may pa-ron)
She can't stand working here / she hates working here.	Elle a horreur de travailler ici. (ell a o-rurr duh trav-eye-ay ee-see)
I was	J'étais (zhet-ay)
dictionary	dictionnaire (dik-syon-air)
revolutionary	révolutionnaire (ray-vol-oos-yon-air)
vocabulary	vocabulaire (voe-kab-you-laire)
I was ordinary.	J'étais ordinaire. (zhet-ay or-din-air)
I was about to... / I was just about to...	J'étais sur le point de... (zhet-ay soor luh pwan duh)
I was about to prepare the dinner / I was just about to prepare the dinner.	J'étais sur le point de préparer le dîner. (zhet-ay soor luh pwan duh pray-par-ay luh din-ay)

I was about to pay the bill.	J'étais sur le point de payer l'addition. (zhet-ay soor luh pwan duh pay-ay la-dis-yon)
I was just about to book a table.	J'étais sur le point de réserver une table. (zhet-ay soor luh pwan duh ray-zurv-ay oon tarb-luh)
You called me / You did call me / You have called me. (formal)	Vous m'avez appelé. (voo ma-vay a-play)
You called me / You did call me / You have called me. (informal)	Tu m'as appelé. (tü ma a-play)
when	quand (kon)
I was just about to book a taxi when you called me.	J'étais sur le point de réserver un taxi quand tu m'as appelé. (zhet-ay soor luh pwan duh ray-zurv-ay urn taxi kon tü ma a-play)
I was about to leave when the telephone rang.	J'étais sur le point de partir quand le téléphone a sonné. (zhet-ay soor luh pwan duh part-ear kon luh tay-lay-fon a sonn-ay)
I was just about to phone you when you knocked at the door. (informal)	J'étais sur le point de te téléphoner quand tu as frappé à la porte. (zhet-ay soor luh pwan duh tuh tay-lay-fone-ay kon tü a frap-ay a la port)
I was just about to order a taxi when it started to rain.	J'étais sur le point de commander un taxi quand il a commencé à pleuvoir. (zhet-ay soor luh pwan duh comm-on-day urn taxi kon deel a com-on-say a pluh-vwar)
so (extremely, very)	tellement (tel-mon)
I am	je suis (zhuh swee)
arrived	arrivé / arrivée (a-reev-ay)
I have arrived / I arrived / I did arrive. (said by a man / boy)	Je suis arrivé. (zhuh swee a-reev-ay)
I have arrived / I arrived / I did arrive. (said by a woman / girl)	Je suis arrivée. (zhuh swee a-reev-ay)
gone	allé / allée (al-ay)

I have gone / I went / I did go. (said by a man / boy)	Je suis allé. (zhuh swee zal-ay)
I have gone / I went / I did go. (said by a woman / girl)	Je suis allée. (zhuh swee zal-ay)
You are (formal)	Vous êtes (voo zet)
You have gone / You went / You did go. (said to a man / boy) – formal	Vous êtes allé. (voo zet al-ay)
You have gone / You went / You did go. (said to a woman / girl) – formal	Vous êtes allée. (voo zet al-ay)
You have arrived / You arrived / You did arrive. (said to a man / boy) – formal	Vous êtes arrivé. (voo zet a-reev-ay)
You have arrived / You arrived / You did arrive. (said to a woman / girl) – formal	Vous êtes arrivée. (voo zet a-reev-ay)
You are (informal)	Tu es (tü ay)
You have arrived / You arrived / You did arrive. (said to a man / boy) – informal	Tu es arrivé. (tü ay a-reev-ay)
You have arrived / You arrived / You did arrive. (said to a woman / girl) – informal	Tu es arrivée. (tü ay a-reev-ay)
I'm sorry.	Je suis désolé / désolée. (zhuh swee dez-oh-lay)
a little / a bit	un peu (urn puh)
I was a little preoccupied / distracted.	J'étais un peu préoccupé / préoccupée. (zhet-ay urn puh pray-ok-oo-pay)
I was in the middle of…	J'étais en train de… (zhet-ay on tran duh)
I'm sorry, I was in the middle of eating when you arrived. (informal)	Je suis désolé / désolée, j'étais en train de manger quand tu es arrivé / arrivée. (zhuh swee dez-oh-lay, zhet-ay on tran duh mon-zhay kon tü ay a-reev-ay)

I'm sorry, I was in the middle of preparing dinner when you arrived so I was a bit distracted. (informal)	Je suis désolé / désolée, j'étais en train de préparer le dîner quand tu es arrivé / arrivée, alors j'étais un peu préoccupé / préoccupée. (zhuh swee dez-oh-lay, zhet-ay on tran duh pray-par-ay luh din-ay kon tü ay a-reev-ay a-law zhet-ay urn puh pray-ok-oo-pay)
I was in the middle of writing to you when my mother arrived. (informal)	J'étais en train de t'écrire quand ma mère est arrivée. (zhet-ay on tran duh tay kreer kon ma maire ay ta-reev-ay)
I was in the middle of leaving the house when you phoned me. (informal)	J'étais en train de partir de la maison quand tu m'as téléphoné. (zhet-ay on tran duh part-ear duh la may-zon kon tü ma tay-lay-fone-ay)
I was in the middle of calling you when your letter arrived. (informal)	J'étais en train de t'appeler quand ta lettre est arrivée. (zhet-ay on tran duh tap-lay kon ta let-ruh ay ta-reev-ay)
July	juillet (zhoo-ee-ay)
in July	en juillet (on zhoo-ee-ay)
I visited Paris in July / I have visited Paris in July / I did visit Paris in July.	J'ai visité Paris en juillet. (zhay visit-ay pa-ree on zhoo-ee-ay)
I'm planning to visit Paris in July.	J'ai l'intention de visiter Paris en juillet. (zhay lon-ton-syon duh visit-ay pa-ree on zhoo-ee-ay)
I'm moving (literally "I dis-household" / "I'm dis-householding")	Je déménage (zhuh day-may-nazh)
I'm moving to France in September.	Je déménage en France en septembre. (zhuh day-may-nazh on fronce on sep-tom-bruh)
because of (literally "at cause of")	à cause de… (a koze duh)
because of you (formal)	à cause de vous (a koze duh voo)
because of you (informal)	à cause de toi (a koze duh twah)
thanks to (literally "grace to")	grâce à… (gras a)
Thanks to me!	Grâce à moi ! (gras a mwah)
Thanks to you! (formal)	Grâce à vous ! (gras a voo)

Thanks to you! (informal)	**Grâce à toi !** (gras a twah)
I'm moving to France in July because of you! (informal)	**Je déménage en France en juillet à cause de toi !** (zhuh day-may-nazh on fronce on zhoo-ee-ay a koze duh twah)
Do you want? (literally "want you?") (formal)	**Voulez-vous ?** (voo-lay voo)
Do you want to prepare the dinner this evening? (formal)	**Voulez-vous préparer le dîner ce soir ?** (voo-lay voo pray-par-ay luh din-ay sir swar)
Do you want to eat something? (formal)	**Voulez-vous manger quelque chose ?** (voo-lay voo mon-zhay kel-kuh shows)
You want (formal)	**Vous voulez** (voo voo-lay)
to say	**dire** (dear)
You mean (literally "you want to say") (formal)	**Vous voulez dire** (voo voolay dear)
I'm moving to France in July because of you! (formal)	**Je déménage en France en juillet à cause de vous !** (zhuh day-may-nazh on fronce on zhoo-ee-ay a koze duh voo)
Because of me? You mean *thanks* to me! (formal)	**À cause de moi ? Vous voulez dire *grâce* à moi !** (a koze duh mwah voo voolay dear gras a mwah)
Actually, I'm moving to Belgium too.	**En fait, je déménage en Belgique aussi.** (on fay, zhuh day-may-nazh on bell-zheek oh-see)
Actually, I'm moving to France next month.	**En fait, je déménage en France le mois prochain.** (on fay, zhuh day-may-nazh on fronce luh mwoire pro-shan)
Actually, I'm going to Paris next year.	**En fait, je vais à Paris l'année prochaine.** (on fay, zhuh vay a pa-ree lan-ay proe-shen)

And it's done! Take a break now before you dive into the final chapter!

The Great Word Robbery

Since the very beginning of the book, I've been giving you examples of how you can rapidly build up your French vocabulary by stealing and converting words from English. Really though, what I've shown you so far has only been the tip of that enormous iceberg I mentioned in the introduction.

I'm now going to give you a far more comprehensive list of word endings that you can use to create thousands of words in French.

Once you've had a read through them, I recommend that you try coming up with a few more examples for each and saying them out loud. The more you do this the more you will find yourself able to instinctively apply the various conversion techniques between English and French.

So, here is the list – it will be your single greatest aid in increasing your French vocabulary:

Words ending in ... in English	Usually become ... in French	Examples
ion	stay the same	transformation information invitation **(1250)**
ic/ical	ique	political = politique typical = typique magic = magique **(750)**
ary	aire	ordinary = ordinaire salary = salaire solitary = solitaire **(400)**
age	stay the same	cage bandage courage **(400)**
ade	stay the same	parade barricade escapade **(150)**
ude	stay the same	attitude gratitude solitude **(100)**
ure	stay the same	agriculture sculpture signature **(300)**

Words ending in … in English	Usually become … in French	Examples
ible/able	stay the same	possible terrible table **(1700)**
ant/ent	stay the same	important intelligent excellent **(1650)**
um	stay the same	album maximum minimum **(600)**
ory	oire	glory = gloire history = histoire victory = victoire **(300)**
id	ide	candid = candide stupid = stupide timid = timide **(300)**
sm	sme	optimism = optimisme pacifism = pacifisme sarcasm = sarcasme **(800)**
ty	té	publicity = publicité activity = activité quality = qualité **(1500)**
or	eur	doctor = docteur actor = acteur pastor = pasteur **(800)**

Words ending in ... in English	Usually become ... in French	Examples
ist	iste	artist = artiste pianist = pianiste fascist = fasciste **(1000)**
ian	ien (m) / ienne (f)	optician = opticien musician = musicien Parisian = Parisien **(250)**
ive	if (m) / ive (f)	active = actif captive = captif massive = massif **(750)**

Word Robbery Total : 13,000

Wow, 13,000 words. Not too shabby in my opinion.

I recommend returning to the list every so often to practise stealing words via the conversion techniques so that every one of them becomes second nature.

CHAPTER 8

When you talk about Paris, you're so enthusiastic

When you talk about Paris, you're so enthusiastic.

Well, you've worked through seven chapters to get to this point. I think it's time to see what you're capable of saying based on all you've learnt with the book.

You are now going to build up to a much longer dialogue than you've done previously *but* much of what you're using will already be familiar to you.

I am sure that you can definitely do this, so let's begin.

What is "I have visited", "I visited", "I did visit"?

J'ai visité
(zhay visit-ay)

How about "I have reserved / booked", "I reserved / booked", "I did reserve / book"?

J'ai réservé
(zhay ray-zurv-ay)

"I have prepared", "I prepared", "I did prepare"?

J'ai préparé
(zhay pray-par-ay)

"I have ordered", "I ordered", "I did order"?

J'ai commandé
(zhay comm-on-day)

"I have paid", "I paid", "I did pay"?

J'ai payé
(zhay pay-ay)

"I have spent", "I spent", "I did spend"?

J'ai passé
(zhay pass-ay)

How would you say "I spent the weekend in France"?

J'ai passé le week-end en France.
(zhay pass-ay luh weekend on fronce)

And how would you say "it was" in French?

c'était
(set-ay)

And so how would you say "it was lovely"?

C'était très agréable.
(set-ay trez ag-ray-arb-luh)

And what was the word for "and" in French?

et
(ay)

Alright, how would you say "I spent the weekend in France and it was lovely"?

J'ai passé le week-end en France et c'était très agréable.
(zhay pass-ay luh weekend on fronce ay set-ay trez ag-ray-arb-luh)

And how would you say "I'm planning to…" in French?

J'ai l'intention de…
(zhay lon-ton-syon duh)

So, how would you say "I'm planning to go back to Paris in May"?

J'ai l'intention de retourner à Paris en mai.
(zhay lon-ton-syon duh ruh-toor-nay a pa-ree on mey)

Now, let's put those two bits together and say "I spent the weekend in France and it was lovely. I'm planning to go back to Paris in May"?

J'ai passé le week-end en France et c'était très agréable. J'ai l'intention de retourner à Paris en mai.
(zhay pass-ay luh weekend on fronce ay set-ay trez ag-ray-arb-luh. zhay lon-ton-syon duh ruh-toor-nay a pa-ree on mey)

Now again, what is "I have"?

J'ai
(zhay)

And "he has"?

Il a
(eel a)

"She has"?

Elle a
(ell a)

"We have"?

Nous avons
(noo za-von)

"They have"?

Ils ont
(eel zon)

"You have" (formal)?

Vous avez
(voo za-vay)

"You have" (informal)?

Tu as
(tü a)

So, how would you say "you are planning to..." (informal)?

Tu as l'intention de…
(tü a lon-ton-syon duh)

And how would you say "you're scared of..." (informal)?

Tu as peur de…
(tü a purr duh)

How about "you're scared of flying" (informal)?

Tu as peur de l'avion.
(tü a purr duh lav-ee-on)

What is "but"?

mais
(mey)

With this in mind, how would you say "But you're scared of flying!"?

Mais tu as peur de l'avion !
(mey tü a purr duh lav-ee-on)

What is "to take"?

prendre
(pron-druh)

So, how would you say "I'm planning to take the Eurostar"?

J'ai l'intention de prendre l'Eurostar.
(zhay lon-ton-syon duh pron-druh luh-roe-star)

What is "so" (meaning "therefore") in French?

alors
(a-law)

How would you say "So I'm planning to take the Eurostar"?

Alors j'ai l'intention de prendre l'Eurostar.
(a-law zhay lon-ton-syon duh pron-druh luh-roe-star)

And again, what is "I'm planning to..."?

J'ai l'intention de...
(zhay lon-ton-syon duh)

And what is "I'm scared of"?

J'ai peur de...
(zhay purr duh)

What about "I can't stand..."?

J'ai horreur de...
(zhay o-rurr duh)

So, how would you say "I can't stand the Eurostar"?

J'ai horreur de l'Eurostar.
(zhay o-rurr duh luh-roe-star)

What is "really"?

vraiment
(vray-mon)

Putting them together, how would you say "Really? I can't stand the Eurostar!"

Vraiment ? J'ai horreur de l'Eurostar !
(vray-mon zhay o-rurr-duh luh-roe-star)

What is "I need..."?

J'ai besoin de...
(zhay burz-won duh)

And how would you say "he needs..." (literally "he has need of...")?

Il a besoin de...
(eel a burz-won duh)

And "she needs..." (literally "she has need of...")?

Elle a besoin de...
(ell a burz-won duh)

How about "we need..."?

Nous avons besoin de...
(noo za-von burz-won duh)

"They need..."?

Ils ont besoin de...
(eel zon burz-won duh)

"You need..." (formal)?

Vous avez besoin de...
(voo za-vay burz-won duh)

"You need..." (informal)?

Tu as besoin de...
(tü a burz-won duh)

Okay, how would you say "you need help, mate!" (informal)?

Tu as besoin d'aide, mon pote !
(tü a burz-won daid mon pote)

Paris

Of course, you might not want to always call someone "mate." You may just want to call them by their names.

So, how would you say "you need help, Louis!"?

Tu as besoin d'aide, Louis!
(tü a burz-won daid, loo-ee)

And let's try the same with a woman, how would you say "you need help, Louise!"?

Tu as besoin d'aide, Louise!
(tü a burz-won daid, loo-eez)

And how would you say "the Eurostar is fantastic"?

L'Eurostar est fantastique.
(luh-roe-star ay fon-tass-teek)

What is "I was just about to…"?

J'étais sur le point de…
(zhet-ay soor luh pwan duh)

And "I was just about to book a table"?

J'étais sur le point de réserver une table.
(zhet-ay soor luh pwan duh ray-zurv-ay oon tarb-luh)

How about "I was just about to book a taxi"?

J'étais sur le point de réserver un taxi.
(zhet-ay soor luh pwan duh ray-zurv-ay urn taxi)

"I was just about to book a room"?

J'étais sur le point de réserver une chambre.
(zhet-ay soor luh pwan duh ray-zurv-ay oon shom-bruh)

"A ticket" in French is:

un billet
(urn bee-yay)

How would you say "I was just about to book a ticket"?

J'étais sur le point de réserver un billet.
(zhet-ay soor luh pwan duh ray-zurv-ay urn bee-yay)

What is the word for "and"?

et
(ay)

So how would you say "…and I was just about to book a ticket"?

…et j'étais sur le point de réserver un billet.
(ay zhet-ay soor luh pwan duh ray-zurv-ay urn bee-yay)

And how you would you say "I arrived" in French?

Je suis arrivé / arrivée.
(zhuh swee a-reev-ay)

How about "you arrived" (informal)?

Tu es arrivé / arrivée.
(tü ay a-reev-ay)

And so, how would you say "…when you arrived" (informal)?

…quand tu es arrivé / arrivée.
(kon tü ay a-reev-ay)

Put these various parts together now and say "…and I was just about to book a ticket when you arrived."

…et j'étais sur le point de réserver un billet quand tu es arrivé / arrivée.
(ay zhet-ay soor luh pwan duh ray-zurv-ay urn bee-yay kon tü ay a-reev-ay)

Now let's put both this and the other parts that came before it together.

Taking your time say: "You need help, Louis! The Eurostar is fantastic and I was just about to book a ticket when you arrived."

Tu as besoin d'aide, Louis! L'Eurostar est fantastique et j'étais sur le point de réserver un billet quand tu es arrivé.
(tü a burz-won daid, loo-ee. luh-roe-star ay fon-tass-teek ay zhet-ay soor luh pwan duh ray-zurv-ay urn bee-yay kon tü ay a-reev-ay)

Notice how, as we're speaking to Louis, "arrived" is written "arrivé."

Let's try this again but this time talking to a woman. Say, "You need help, Louise! The Eurostar is fantastic and I was just about to book a ticket when you arrived."

Tu as besoin d'aide, Louise! L'Eurostar est fantastique et j'étais sur le point de réserver un billet quand tu es arrivée.
(tü a burz-won dai, loo-eez. luh-roe-star ay fon-tass-teek ay zhet-ay soor luh pwan duh ray-zurv-ay urn bee-yay kon tü ay a-reev-ay)

Now, how would someone say "really?" in response to that?

Vraiment ?
(vray-mon)

And once more, what is "I was just about to…"?

J'étais sur le point de…
(zhet-ay soor luh pwan duh)

And how would you say "I was in the middle of…"?

J'étais en train de…
(zhet-ay on tran duh)

So, how would you say "I was in the middle of booking a ticket"?

J'étais en train de réserver un billet.
(zhet-ay on tran duh ray-zurv-ay urn bee-yay)

And how would you say "…when you knocked at the door"?

…quand tu as frappé à la porte
(kon tü a frap-ay a la port)

Let's now combine these elements and say "I was in the middle of booking a ticket when you knocked at the door.":

J'étais en train de réserver un billet quand tu as frappé à la porte.
(zhet-ay on tran duh ray-zurv-ay urn bee-yay kon tü a frap-ay a la port)

How would someone reply to this saying "oh, sorry"?

Oh, désolé / désolée.
(oh dez-oh-lay)

What is "I feel like…" or "I fancy…"?

J'ai envie de…
(zhay on-vee duh)

How about "I feel like visiting Paris?"

J'ai envie de visiter Paris.
(zhay on-vee duh visit-ay pa-ree)

What is "too" or "also" in French?

aussi
(oh-see)

So, how would you say "I feel like visiting Paris too"?

J'ai envie de visiter Paris aussi.
(zhay on-vee duh visit-ay pa-ree oh-see)

What is "actually" or "in fact" in French?

en fait
(on fay)

If you wanted to give a fuller answer, how would you say "Oh, sorry. Actually, I feel like visiting Paris too."?

Oh, désolé / désolée. En fait, j'ai envie de visiter Paris aussi.
(oh dez-oh-lay. on fay zhay on-vee duh visit-ay pa-ree oh-see)

How would someone reply to that by saying "Really?"?

Vraiment ?
(vray-mon)

What is "because of…"?

à cause de…
(a koze duh)

And how would you say "because of you" (formal)?

à cause de vous
(a koze duh voo)

And how about "because of me"?

à cause de moi
(a koze duh mwah)

And what about "because of you" (informal)?

à cause de toi
(a koze duh twah)

So, if "à cause de toi" means "because of you", which of those words means "of "?

de
(duh)

What is "to speak" or "to talk" in French?

parler
(par-lay)

"You speak" or "you talk" (informal) in French is:

tu parles
(tü parl)

To say "you speak about" or "you talk about" in French, you will literally say "you speak of " or "you talk of."

So how would you say "you talk about" (informal) – (literally "you speak of / you talk of ")?

tu parles de
(tü parl duh)

Now how would you say "you talk about Paris" (informal)?

Tu parles de Paris.
(tü parl duh pa-ree)

How about "when you talk about Paris" (informal)?

quand tu parles de Paris
(kon tü parl duh pa-ree)

What is "you are" (informal)?

Tu es
(tü ay)

And what is "enthusiastic"?

enthousiaste
(on-tooze-ee-ast)

And what is "so" in the sense of "extremely" or "very"?

tellement
(tel-mon)

How would you say "you are so enthusiastic" (informal)?

Tu es tellement enthousiaste.
(tü ay tel-mon on-tooze-ee-ast)

If you want to reply to something you feel is a
compliment, you can, of course, say "thank you".
Many people will be already familiar with the French
word for "thank you", which is:

merci
(mare-see)

If you want to make that more emphatic, you can say "wow, thank you!"
Wow in French is written as:

Ouahou
(wow)

So, how would you say "wow, thank you!"?

Ouahou, merci !
(wow mare-see)

And once again, what is "you speak" or "you talk" (informal) in French?

tu parles
(tü parl)

And how would you say "you speak about" or "you talk about" (informal) –
(literally "you speak of / you talk of ")?

tu parles de
(tü parl duh)

And how would you you say "you talk about Paris" (informal)?

tu parles de Paris
(tü parl duh pa-ree)

And what about "when you talk about Paris" (informal)?

quand tu parles de Paris
(kon tü parl duh pa-ree)

And again, how would you say "you are so enthusiastic" (informal)?

Tu es tellement enthousiaste.
(tü ay tel-mon on-tooze-ee-ast)

Putting this all together now, say "When you talk about Paris you are so enthusiastic."

Quand tu parles de Paris tu es tellement enthousiaste.
(kon tü parl duh pa-ree tü ay tel-mon on-tooze-ee-ast)

How would the person you were talking to reply "Wow, thanks!"?

Ouahou, merci !
(wow, mare-see)

If by your enthusiasm you actually managed to persuade someone that they also wanted to go to Paris, they might say "Wow, let's go!"

"Let's go" is:

Allons-y !
(a-lon-zee)

So, finally, how would you say "Wow, thanks! Let's go!"?

Ouahou, merci ! Allons-y !
(wow mare-see. a-lon-zee)

Alright, I think it's time you had a crack at the long dialogue I mentioned at the beginning of the chapter.

Try going through it, slowly the first couple of times and then, once you feel confident enough, see if you can get to the point where you can construct the entire dialogue without needing to pause. It will take a fair amount of practice but, every time you go through it, it will greatly benefit your French.

As you will already be finding, I hope, the more you practise constructing these sentences, the more naturally and fluidly they come out.

Are you ready then? Take your time and off you go with the final dialogue:

I spent the weekend in France and it was lovely. I'm planning to go back to Paris in May.
J'ai passé le week-end en France et c'était très agréable. J'ai l'intention de retourner à Paris en mai.
(zhay pass-ay luh weekend on fronce ay set-ay trez ag-ray-arb-luh.
zhay lon-ton-syon duh ruh-toor-nay a pa-ree on mey)

But you're scared of flying!
Mais tu as peur de l'avion !
(mey tü a purr-duh lav-ee-on)

Yes, so I'm planning to take the Eurostar.
Oui, alors j'ai l'intention de prendre l'Eurostar.
(wee, a-law zhay lon-ton-syon duh pron-druh luh-roe-star)

Really? I can't stand the Eurostar.
Vraiment ? J'ai horreur de l'Eurostar !
(vray-mon zhay o-rurr-duh luh-roe-star)

You need help, Louis / Louise! The Eurostar is fantastic and I was just about to book a ticket when you arrived.
Tu as besoin d'aide, Louis / Louise ! L'Eurostar est fantastique et j'étais sur le point de réserver un billet quand tu es arrivé / arrivée.
(tü a burz-won daid loo-ee / loo-eez. luh-roe-star ay fon-tass-teek ay zhet-ay soor luh pwan duh ray-zurv-ay urn bee-yay kon tü ay a-reev-ay)

Really?
Vraiment ?
(vray-mon)

Yes, I was in the middle of booking a ticket when you knocked at the door.
Oui, j'étais en train de réserver un billet quand tu as frappé à la porte.
(wee, zhet-ay on tran duh ray-zurv-ay urn bee-yay kon tü a frap-ay a la port)

Oh, sorry. Actually, I feel like visiting Paris too.
Oh, désolé / désolée. En fait, j'ai envie de visiter Paris aussi.
(*oh dez-oh-lay. on fay zhay on-vee duh visit-ay pa-ree oh-see*)

Really?
Vraiment ?
(*vray-mon*)

Yes – because of you.
Oui, à cause de toi.
(*wee, a koze duh twah*)

Because of me? Really?
À cause de moi ? Vraiment ?
(*a koze duh mwah? vray-mon?*)

Yes, when you talk about Paris you're so enthusiastic.
Oui, quand tu parles de Paris tu es tellement enthousiaste.
(*wee, kon tü parl duh pa-ree tü ay tel-mon on-tooze-ee-ast*)

Wow, thanks! Let's go!
Ouahou, merci ! Allons-y !
(*wow mare-see. a-lon-zee*)

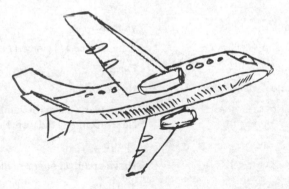

Well, this is your final checklist. Unlike the ones that came before it, however, you are not finished with this one until you can go the whole way through it without making a single mistake.

This doesn't mean that making mistakes when you go through it is a bad thing. It's just that I want you to return to it multiple times so that going through the list becomes so easy that you can do it without making a single error.

When you can, it means you have really learnt what I wanted to teach you in these pages.

Now, get to it!

le week-end (luh weekend)	the weekend
pragmatique (prag-ma-teek)	pragmatic
excentrique (ex-son-treek)	eccentric
cynique (sin-eek)	cynical
théologique (tay-ol-oh-zheek)	theological
enthousiaste (on-tooze-ee-ast)	enthusiastic
J'ai (zhay)	I have
visité (visit-ay)	visited
J'ai visité (zhay visit-ay)	I have visited / I visited / I did visit
Paris (pa-ree)	Paris
Notre-Dame (not-re darm)	Notre-Dame
J'ai visité Notre-Dame. (zhay visit-ay not-re darm)	I have visited Notre-Dame / I visited Notre-Dame / I did visit Notre-Dame.
passé (pass-ay)	spent
J'ai passé (zhay pass-ay)	I have spent / I spent / I did spend
Vous avez (voo za-vay)	You have
Vous avez passé (voo za-vay pass-ay)	You have spent / You spent / You did spend
Nous avons (noo za-von)	We have

Nous avons passé (noo za-von pass-ay)	We have spent / We spent / We did spend
septembre (sep-tom-bruh)	September
Noël (no-ell)	Christmas
à Paris (a pa-ree)	in Paris
en France (on fronce)	in France
en Suisse (on swees)	in Switzerland
Nous avons passé Noël en Suisse. (noo za-von pass-ay no-ell on swees)	We have spent Christmas in Switzerland / We spent Christmas in Switzerland / We did spend Christmas in Switzerland.
Vous avez passé septembre en France. (voo za-vay pass-ay sep-tom-bruh on fronce)	You have spent September in France / You spent September in France / You did spend September in France.
et (ay)	and
c'était (set-ay)	it was
C'était fantastique. (set-ay fon-tass-teek)	It was fantastic.
très agréable (trez ag-ray-arb-luh)	lovely / very agreeable
C'était très agréable. (set-ay trez ag-ray-arb-luh)	It was lovely. / It was very agreeable.
J'ai passé le week-end à Paris… et c'était très agréable. (zhay pass-ay luh weekend a pa-ree… ay set-ay trez ag-ray-arb-luh)	I spent the weekend in Paris… and it was lovely.
expression (ex-press-yon)	expression
version (vur-syon)	version
opinion (oh-pin-yon)	opinion
invité (earn-vit-ay)	invited
préparé (pray-par-ay)	prepared
réservé (ray-zurv-ay)	reserved / booked
commandé (comm-on-day)	ordered
payé (pay-ay)	paid
fait (fay)	done

l'addition (la-dis-yon)	the bill
le dîner (luh din-ay)	the dinner
le rosbif (luh ros-beef)	the roast beef
une table (oon tarb-luh)	a table
une chambre (oon shom-bruh)	a room
un taxi (urn taxi)	a taxi
J'ai préparé le dîner. (zhay pray-par-ay luh din-ay)	I have prepared the dinner / I prepared the dinner / I did prepare the dinner.
J'ai commandé le rosbif pour le dîner. (zhay comm-on-day luh ros-beef poor luh din-ay)	I have ordered roast beef for dinner / I ordered roast beef for dinner / I did order roast beef for dinner.
J'ai réservé une table pour vous. (zhay ray-zurv-ay oon tarb-luh poor voo)	I have booked a table for you / I booked a table for you / I did book a table for you.
Elle a (ell a)	She has
Elle a réservé une table pour ce soir. (ell a ray-zurv-ay oon tarb-luh poor sir swar)	She has booked / reserved a table for this evening – She booked / reserved a table for this evening – She did book / reserve a table for this evening.
Il a (eel a)	He has
Il a réservé une chambre pour deux personnes. (eel a ray-zurv-ay oon shom-bruh poor duh purse-on)	He has booked / reserved a room for two people – He booked / reserved a room for two people – He did book / reserve a room for two people.
Nous avons réservé un taxi pour vous. (noo za-von ray-zur-vay urn taxi poor voo)	We have booked a taxi for you / We booked a taxi for you / We did book a taxi for you.
Nous avons payé l'addition. (noo za-von pay-ay la-dis-yon)	We paid the bill / We have paid the the bill / We did pay the bill.
Qu'est-ce que ? (kess-kuh)	What? / What is it that?
Qu'est-ce que vous avez préparé ? (kess-kuh voo za-vay pray-par-ay)	What have you prepared? / What did you prepare? (literally "What is it that you have prepared?")

Qu'est-ce que vous avez fait ? (kess-kuh voo za-vay fay)	What have you done? / What did you do? (literally "What is it that you have done?")
J'ai réservé une table, commandé le dîner et puis payé l'addition. Qu'est-ce que vous avez fait ? (zhay ray-zurv-ay oon tarb-luh, comm-on-day luh din-ay ay pwee pay-ay la-dis-yon. kess-kuh voo za-vay fay)	I booked a table, ordered dinner and then paid the bill. What did you do?
J'ai l'intention de… (zhay lon-ton-syon duh)	I'm planning to… (literally "I have the intention of…")
J'ai l'intention de retourner en France en mai. (zhay lon-ton-syon duh ruh-toor-nay on fronce on mey)	I'm planning to go back to France in May.
J'ai peur de… (zhay purr duh)	I'm scared of… (literally "I have fear of…")
J'ai peur de retourner en France en septembre. (zhay purr duh ruh-toor-nay on fronce on sep-tom-bruh)	I'm scared of going back to France in September.
Vraiment ? (vray-mon)	Really?
alors (a-law)	so (therefore)
mais (may)	but
J'ai envie de… (zhay on-vee duh)	I feel like… / I fancy… (literally "I have envy of…")
Oui, j'ai envie de retourner à Paris mais j'ai peur de l'avion, alors j'ai l'intention de prendre l'Eurostar. (wee zhay on-vee duh ruh-toor-nay a pa-ree may zhay purr duh lav-ee-on, a-law zhay lon-ton-syon duh pron-druh luh-roe-star)	Yes, I feel like going back to Paris but I'm scared of flying, so I'm planning to take the Eurostar.
J'ai envie d'acheter quelque chose ce matin. (zhay on-vee dash-tay kel-kuh shows sir mat-an)	I feel like / fancy buying something this morning.

Il a envie de lire quelque chose cet après-midi. (eel a on-vee duh leer kel-kuh shows set ap-ray mi-dee)	He feels like / fancies reading something this afternoon.
Ils ont (eel zon)	They have
Ils ont envie de manger quelque chose ce soir. (eel zon on-vee duh mon-zhay kel-kuh shows sir swar)	They feel like eating something this evening.
J'ai besoin de… (zhay burz-won duh)	I need… (literally "I have need of…")
J'ai besoin de parler français. (zhay burz-won duh par-lay fron-say)	I need to speak French.
J'ai besoin d'un taxi. (zhay burz-won durn taxi)	I need a taxi.
J'ai besoin d'une chambre. (zhay burz-won doon shom-bruh)	I need a room.
J'ai besoin d'aide. (zhay burz-won daid)	I need help.
Tu as besoin d'aide, mon pote ! (tü a burz-won daid mon pote)	You need help, mate!
J'ai horreur de… (zhay o-rurr duh)	I can't stand… / I hate… (literally "I have horror of…")
J'ai horreur de l'avion ! (zhay o-rurr duh lav-ee-on)	I can't stand flying! / I can't stand planes! / I hate flying!
J'ai horreur de manger avec mes beaux-parents. (zhay o-rurr duh mon-zhay av-eck may boe pa-ron)	I can't stand eating with my in-laws / I hate eating with my in-laws.
Nous avons horreur de manger avec mes parents. (noo za-von o-rurr duh mon-zhay av-eck may pa-ron)	We can't stand eating with my parents / We hate eating with my parents.
Elle a horreur de travailler ici. (ella o-rurr duh trav-eye-ay ee-see)	She can't stand working here / she hates working here.
J'étais (zhet-ay)	I was
extraordinaire (ex-trah-ord-in-air)	extraordinary
imaginaire (eem-azh-een-air)	imaginary
nécessaire (ness-ess-air)	necessary
J'étais ordinaire (zhet-ay ord-in-air)	I was ordinary

J'étais sur le point de… (zhet-ay soor luh pwan duh)	I was about to… / I was just about to… (literally "I was on the point of…")
J'étais sur le point de préparer le dîner. (zhet-ay soor luh pwan duh pray-par-ay luh din-ay)	I was about to prepare the dinner / I was just about to prepare the dinner.
J'étais sur le point de payer l'addition. (zhet-ay soor luh pwan duh pay-ay la-dis-yon)	I was about to pay the bill.
J'étais sur le point de réserver une table. (zhet-ay soor luh pwan duh ray-zurv-ay oon tarb-luh)	I was just about to book a table.
Vous m'avez appelé. (voo ma-vay a-play)	You called me / You did call me / You have called me. (formal)
Tu m'as appelé. (tü ma a-play)	You called me / You did call me / You have called me. (informal)
quand (kon)	when
J'étais sur le point de réserver un taxi quand tu m'as appelé. (zhet-ay soor luh pwan duh ray-zurv-ay urn taxi kon tü ma a-play)	I was just about to book a taxi when you called me.
J'étais sur le point de partir quand le téléphone a sonné. (zhet-ay soor luh pwan duh part-ear kon luh tay-lay-fon a sonn-ay)	I was about to leave when the telephone rang.
J'étais sur le point de te téléphoner quand tu as frappé à la porte. (zhet-ay soor luh pwan duh tuh tay-lay-fone-ay kon tü a frap-ay a la port)	I was just about to phone you when you knocked at the door. (informal)
J'étais sur le point de commander un taxi quand il a commencé à pleuvoir. (zhet-ay soor luh pwan duh comm-on-day urn taxi kon deel a com-on-say a pluh-vwar)	I was just about to order a taxi when it started to rain.
tellement (tel-mon)	so (extremely, very)
je suis (zhuh swee)	I am
arrivé / arrivée (a-reev-ay)	arrived

Je suis arrivé. (zhuh swee a-reev-ay)	I have arrived / I arrived / I did arrive. (said by a man / boy)
Je suis arrivée. (zhuh swee a-reev-ay)	I have arrived / I arrived / I did arrive. (said by a woman / girl)
allé / allée (al-ay)	gone
Je suis allé. (zhuh swee zal-ay)	I have gone / I went / I did go. (said by a man / boy)
Je suis allée. (zhuh swee zal-ay)	I have gone / I went / I did go. (said by a woman / girl)
Vous êtes (voo zet)	You are (formal)
Vous êtes allé. (voo zet al-ay)	You have gone / You went / You did go. (said to a man / boy) – formal
Vous êtes allée. (voo zet al-ay)	You have gone / You went / You did go. (said to a woman / girl) – formal
Vous êtes arrivé. (voo zet a-reev-ay)	You have arrived / You arrived / You did arrive. (said to a man / boy) – formal
Vous êtes arrivée. (voo zet a-reev-ay)	You have arrived / You arrived / You did arrive. (said to a woman / girl) – formal
Tu es (tü ay)	You are (informal)
Tu es arrivé. (tü ay a-reev-ay)	You have arrived / You arrived / You did arrive. (said to a man / boy) – informal
Tu es arrivée. (tü ay a-reev-ay)	You have arrived / You arrived / You did arrive. (said to a woman / girl) – informal
Je suis désolé / désolée. (zhuh swee dez-oh-lay)	I'm sorry.
un peu (urn puh)	a little / a bit
J'étais un peu préoccupé / préoccupée. (zhet-ay urn puh pray-ok-oo-pay)	I was a little preoccupied / distracted.
J'étais en train de… (zhet-ay on tran duh)	I was in the middle of… (literally "I was in train of…")

Je suis désolé / désolée, j'étais en train de manger quand tu es arrivé / arrivée. (zhuh swee dez-oh-lay, zhet-ay on tran duh mon-zhay kon tü ay a-reev-ay)	I'm sorry, I was in the middle of eating when you arrived. (informal)
Je suis désolé / désolée, j'étais en train de préparer le dîner quand tu es arrivé / arrivée, alors j'étais un peu préoccupé / préoccupée. (zhuh swee dez-oh-lay, zhet-ay on tran duh pray-par-ay luh din-ay kon tü ay a-reev-ay a-law zhet-ay urn puh pray-ok-oo-pay)	I'm sorry, I was in the middle of preparing dinner when you arrived so I was a bit distracted. (informal)
J'étais en train de t'écrire quand ma mère est arrivée. (zhet-ay on tran duh tay kreer kon ma maire ay ta-reev-ay)	I was in the middle of writing to you when my mother arrived. (informal)
J'étais en train de partir de la maison quand tu m'as téléphoné. (zhet-ay on tran duh part-ear duh la may-zon kon tü ma tay-lay-fone-ay)	I was in the middle of leaving the house when you phoned me. (informal)
J'étais en train de t'appeler quand ta lettre est arrivée. (zhet-ay on tran duh tap-lay kon ta let-ruh ay ta reev ay)	I was in the middle of calling you when your letter arrived. (informal)
juillet (zhoo-ee-ay)	July
en juillet (on zhoo-ee-ay)	in July
J'ai visité Paris en juillet. (zhay visit-ay pa-ree on zhoo-ee-ay)	I visited Paris in July / I have visited Paris in July / I did visit Paris in July.
J'ai l'intention de visiter Paris en juillet. (zhay lon-ton-syon duh visit-ay pa-ree on zhoo-ee-ay)	I'm planning to visit Paris in July.
Je déménage (zhuh day-may-nazh)	I'm moving (literally "I dis-household" / "I'm dis-householding")
Je déménage en France en septembre. (zhuh day-may-nazh on fronce on sep-tom-bruh)	I'm moving to France in September.
à cause de... (a koze duh)	because of (literally "at cause of")

à cause de vous (a koze duh voo)	because of you (formal)
à cause de toi (a koze duh twah)	because of you (informal)
grâce à… (gras a)	thanks to (literally "grace to")
Grâce à moi ! (gras a mwah)	Thanks to me!
Grâce à vous ! (gras a voo)	Thanks to you! (formal)
Grâce à toi ! (gras a twah)	Thanks to you! (informal)
Je déménage en France en juillet à cause de toi ! (zhuh day-may-nazh on fronce on zhoo-ee-ay a koze duh twah)	I'm moving to France in July because of you! (informal)
Voulez-vous ? (voo-lay voo)	Do you want? (literally "want you?") – (formal)
Voulez-vous préparer le dîner ce soir ? (voo-lay voo pray-par-ay luh din-ay sir swar)	Do you want to prepare the dinner this evening? (formal)
Voulez-vous manger quelque chose ? (voo-lay voo mon-zhay kel-kuh shows)	Do you want to eat something? (formal)
Vous voulez (voo voo-lay)	You want (formal)
dire (dear)	to say
Vous voulez dire (voo voolay dear)	You mean (literally "you want to say") – (formal)
Je déménage en France en juillet à cause de vous ! (zhuh day-may-nazh on fronce on zhoo-ee-ay a koze duh voo)	I'm moving to France in July because of you! (formal)
À cause de moi ? Vous voulez dire grâce à moi ! (a koze duh mwah voo voolay dear gras a mwah)	Because of me? You mean *thanks to me!* (formal)
En fait, je déménage en Belgique aussi. (on fay, zhuh day-may-nazh on bell-zheek oh-see)	Actually, I'm moving to Belgium too.
En fait, je déménage en France le mois prochain. (on fay, zhuh day-may-nazh on fronce luh mwoire pro-shan)	Actually, I'm moving to France next month.

En fait, je vais à Paris l'année prochaine. (on fay, zhuh vay a pa-ree lan-ay proe-shen)	Actually, I'm going to Paris next year.
un billet (urn bee-yay)	a ticket
ouahou (wow)	wow
merci (mare-see)	thanks
Allons-y ! (a-lon-zee)	Let's go!
Tu as besoin d'aide, Louis / Louise ! L'Eurostar est fantastique et j'étais sur le point de réserver un billet quand tu es arrivé / arrivée. (tü a burz-won daid loo-ee / loo-eez. luh-roe-star ay fon-tass-teek ay zhet-ay soor luh pwan duh ray-zurv ay urn bee-yay kon tü ay a-reev-ay)	You need help, Louis / Louise! The Eurostar is fantastic and I was just about to book a ticket when you arrived. (informal)
Oh, désolé / désolée. En fait, j'ai envie de visiter Paris aussi. (oh dez-oh-lay. on fay zhay on-vee duh visit-ay pa-ree oh-see)	Oh, sorry. Actually, I feel like visiting Paris too.
Oui, quand tu parles de Paris tu es tellement enthousiaste. (wee, kon tü parl duh pa-ree tü ay tel-mon on-tooze-ee-ast)	Yes, when you talk about Paris you're so enthusiastic. (informal)
Ouahou, merci ! Allons-y ! (wow mare-see. a-lon-zee)	Wow, thanks! Let's go!

Having worked your way through the French-to-English list above without making any mistakes, you will now want to get to the point where you can also work through the English-to-French list without making any mistakes. You should feel free to do this over several days or even weeks if you feel you need to. Just take your time and work at it until constructing the sentences and recalling the words become second nature to you.

the weekend	le week-end (luh weekend)
pragmatic	pragmatique (prag-ma-teek)
eccentric	excentrique (ex-son-treek)
cynical	cynique (sin-eek)
theological	théologique (tay-ol-oh-zheek)
enthusiastic	enthousiaste (on-tooze-ee-ast)
I have	J'ai (zhay)
visited	visité (visit-ay)
I have visited / I visited / I did visit	J'ai visité (zhay visit-ay)
Paris	Paris (pa-ree)
Notre-Dame	Notre-Dame (not-re darm)
I have visited Notre-Dame / I visited Notre-Dame / I did visit Notre-Dame.	J'ai visité Notre-Dame. (zhay visit-ay not-re darm)
spent	passé (pass-ay)
I have spent / I spent / I did spend	J'ai passé (zhay pass-ay)
You have	Vous avez (voo za-vay)
You have spent / You spent / You did spend	Vous avez passé (voo za-vay pass-ay)
We have	Nous avons (noo za-von)
We have spent / We spent / We did spend	Nous avons passé (noo za-von pass-ay)
September	septembre (sep-tom-bruh)
Christmas	Noël (no-ell)
in Paris	à Paris (a pa-ree)
in France	en France (on fronce)
in Switzerland	en Suisse (on swees)
We have spent Christmas in Switzerland / We spent Christmas in Switzerland / We did spend Christmas in Switzerland.	Nous avons passé Noël en Suisse. (noo za-von pass-ay no-ell on swees)
You have spent September in France / You spent September in France / You did spend September in France.	Vous avez passé septembre en France. (voo za-vay pass-ay sep-tom-bruh on fronce)

and	et (ay)
it was	c'était (set-ay)
It was fantastic.	C'était fantastique. (set-ay fon-tass-teek)
lovely / very agreeable	très agréable (trez ag-ray-arb-luh)
It was lovely. / It was very agreeable.	C'était très agréable. (set-ay trez ag-ray-arb-luh)
I spent the weekend in Paris… and it was lovely.	J'ai passé le week-end à Paris… et c'était très agréable. (zhay pass-ay luh weekend a pa-ree… ay set-ay trez ag-ray-arb-luh)
expression	expression (ex-press-yon)
version	version (vur-syon)
opinion	opinion (oh-pin-yon)
invited	invité (earn-vit-ay)
prepared	préparé (pray-par-ay)
reserved / booked	réservé (ray-zurv-ay)
ordered	commandé (comm-on-day)
paid	payé (pay-ay)
done	fait (fay)
the bill	l'addition (la-dis-yon)
the dinner	le dîner (luh din-ay)
the roast beef	le rosbif (luh ros-beef)
a table	une table (oon tarb-luh)
a room	une chambre (oon shom-bruh)
a taxi	un taxi (urn taxi)
I have prepared the dinner / I prepared the dinner / I did prepare the dinner.	J'ai préparé le dîner. (zhay pray-par-ay luh din-ay)
I have ordered roast beef for dinner / I ordered roast beef for dinner / I did order roast beef for dinner.	J'ai commandé le rosbif pour le dîner. (zhay comm-on-day luh ros-beef poor luh din-ay)

I have booked a table for you / I booked a table for you / I did book a table for you. (formal)	J'ai réservé une table pour vous. (zhay ray-zurv-ay oon tarb-luh poor voo)
She has	Elle a (ell a)
She has booked / reserved a table for this evening – She booked / reserved a table for this evening – She did book / reserve a table for this evening.	Elle a réservé une table pour ce soir. (ell a ray-zurv-ay oon tarb-luh poor sir swar)
He has	Il a (eel a)
He has booked / reserved a room for two people – He booked / reserved a room for two people – He did book / reserve a room for two people.	Il a réservé une chambre pour deux personnes. (eel a ray-zurv-ay oon shom-bruh poor duh purse-on)
We have booked a taxi for you / We booked a taxi for you / We did book a taxi for you. (formal)	Nous avons réservé un taxi pour vous. (noo za-von ray-zur-vay urn taxi poor voo)
We paid the bill / We have paid the the bill / We did pay the bill.	Nous avons payé l'addition. (noo za-von pay-ay la-dis-yon)
What? / What is it that?	Qu'est-ce que ? (kess-kuh)
What have you prepared? / What did you prepare?	Qu'est-ce que vous avez préparé ? (kess-kuh voo za-vay pray-par-ay)
What have you done? / What did you do?	Qu'est-ce que vous avez fait ? (kess-kuh voo za-vay fay)
I booked a table, ordered dinner and then paid the bill. What did you do?	J'ai réservé une table, commandé le dîner et puis payé l'addition. Qu'est-ce que vous avez fait ? (zhay ray-zurv-ay oon tarb-luh, comm-on-day luh din-ay ay pwee pay-ay la-dis-yon. kess-kuh voo za-vay fay)
I'm planning to…	J'ai l'intention de… (zhay lon-ton-syon duh)
I'm planning to go back to France in May.	J'ai l'intention de retourner en France en mai. (zhay lon-ton-syon duh ruh-toor-nay on fronce on mey)
I'm scared of…	J'ai peur de… (zhay purr duh)

I'm scared of going back to France in September.	J'ai peur de retourner en France en septembre. (zhay purr duh ruh-toor-nay on fronce on sep-tom-bruh)
Really?	Vraiment? (vray-mon)
so (therefore)	alors (a-law)
but	mais (may)
I feel like… / I fancy…	J'ai envie de… (zhay on-vee duh)
Yes, I feel like going back to Paris but I'm scared of flying, so I'm planning to take the Eurostar.	Oui, j'ai envie de retourner à Paris mais j'ai peur de l'avion, alors j'ai l'intention de prendre l'Eurostar. (wee zhay on-vee duh ruh-toor-nay a pa-ree may zhay purr duh lav-ee-on, a-law zhay lon-ton-syon duh pron-druh luh-roe-star)
I feel like / fancy buying something this morning.	J'ai envie d'acheter quelque chose ce matin. (zhay on-vee dash-tay kel-kuh shows sir mat-an)
He feels like / fancies reading something this afternoon.	Il a envie de lire quelque chose cet après-midi. (eel a on-vee duh leer kel-kuh shows set ap-ray mi-dee)
They have	Ils ont (eel zon)
They feel like eating something this evening.	Ils ont envie de manger quelque chose ce soir. (eel zon on-vee duh mon-zhay kel-kuh shows sir swar)
I need…	J'ai besoin de… (zhay burz-won duh)
I need to speak French.	J'ai besoin de parler français. (zhay burz-won duh par-lay fron-say)
I need a taxi.	J'ai besoin d'un taxi. (zhay burz-won durn taxi)
I need a room.	J'ai besoin d'une chambre. (zhay burz-won doon shom-bruh)
I need help.	J'ai besoin d'aide. (zhay burz-won daid)
You need help, mate! (informal)	Tu as besoin d'aide, mon pote ! (tü a burz-won daid mon pote)

I can't stand… / I hate…	J'ai horreur de… (zhay o-rurr duh)
I can't stand flying! / I can't stand planes! / I hate flying!	J'ai horreur de l'avion ! (zhay o-rurr duh lav-ee-on)
I can't stand eating with my in-laws / I hate eating with my in-laws.	J'ai horreur de manger avec mes beaux-parents. (zhay o-rurr duh mon-zhay av-eck may boe pa-ron)
We can't stand eating with my parents / We hate eating with my parents.	Nous avons horreur de manger avec mes parents. (noo za-von o-rurr duh mon-zhay av-eck may pa-ron)
She can't stand working here / she hates working here.	Elle a horreur de travailler ici. (ell a o-rurr duh trav-eye-ay ee-see)
I was	J'étais (zhet-ay)
extraordinary	extraordinaire (ex-trah-ord-in-air)
imaginary	imaginaire (eem-azh-een-air)
necessary	nécessaire (ness-ess-air)
I was ordinary	J'étais ordinaire (zhet-ay ord-in-air)
I was about to… / I was just about to…	J'étais sur le point de… (zhet-ay soor luh pwan duh)
I was about to prepare the dinner / I was just about to prepare the dinner.	J'étais sur le point de préparer le dîner. (zhet-ay soor luh pwan duh pray-par-ay luh din-ay)
I was about to pay the bill.	J'étais sur le point de payer l'addition. (zhet-ay soor luh pwan duh pay-ay la-dis-yon)
I was just about to book a table.	J'étais sur le point de réserver une table. (zhet-ay soor luh pwan duh ray-zurv-ay oon tarb-luh)
You called me / You did call me / You have called me. (formal)	Vous m'avez appelé. (voo ma-vay a-play)
You called me / You did call me / You have called me. (informal)	Tu m'as appelé. (tü ma a-play)
when	quand (kon)
I was just about to book a taxi when you called me.	J'étais sur le point de réserver un taxi quand tu m'as appelé. (zhet-ay soor luh pwan duh ray-zurv-ay urn taxi kon tü ma a-play)

I was about to leave when the telephone rang.	J'étais sur le point de partir quand le téléphone a sonné. (zhet-ay soor luh pwan duh part-ear kon luh tay-lay-fon a sonn-ay)
I was just about to phone you when you knocked at the door. (informal)	J'étais sur le point de te téléphoner quand tu as frappé à la porte. (zhet-ay soor luh pwan duh tuh tay-lay-fone-ay kon tü a frap-ay a la port)
I was just about to order a taxi when it started to rain.	J'étais sur le point de commander un taxi quand il a commencé à pleuvoir. (zhet-ay soor luh pwan duh comm-on-day urn taxi kon deel a com-on-say a pluh-vwar)
so (extremely, very)	tellement (tel-mon)
I am	je suis (zhuh swee)
arrived	arrivé / arrivée (a-reev-ay)
I have arrived / I arrived / I did arrive. (said by a man / boy)	Je suis arrivé. (zhuh swee a-reev-ay)
I have arrived / I arrived / I did arrive. (said by a woman / girl)	Je suis arrivée. (zhuh swee a-reev-ay)
gone	allé / allée (al-ay)
I have gone / I went / I did go (said by a man / boy)	Je suis allé. (zhuh swee zal-ay)
I have gone / I went / I did go. (said by a woman / girl)	Je suis allée. (zhuh swee zal-ay)
You are (formal)	Vous êtes (voo zet)
You have gone / You went / You did go. (said to a man / boy) – formal	Vous êtes allé. (voo zet al-ay)
You have gone / You went / You did go. (said to a woman / girl) – formal	Vous êtes allée. (voo zet al-ay)
You have arrived / You arrived / You did arrive. (said to a man / boy) – formal	Vous êtes arrivé. (voo zet a-reev-ay)
You have arrived / You arrived / You did arrive. (said to a woman / girl) – formal	Vous êtes arrivée. (voo zet a-reev-ay)

You are (informal)	Tu es (tü ay)
You have arrived / You arrived / You did arrive. (said to a man / boy) – informal	Tu es arrivé. (tü ay a-reev-ay)
You have arrived / You arrived / You did arrive. (said to a woman / girl) – informal	Tu es arrivée. (tü ay a-reev-ay)
I'm sorry.	Je suis désolé / désolée. (zhuh swee dez-oh-lay)
a little / a bit	un peu (urn puh)
I was a little preoccupied / distracted.	J'étais un peu préoccupé / préoccupée. (zhet-ay urn puh pray-ok-oo-pay)
I was in the middle of…	J'étais en train de… (zhet-ay on tran duh)
I'm sorry, I was in the middle of eating when you arrived. (informal)	Je suis désolé / désolée, j'étais en train de manger quand tu es arrivé / arrivée. (zhuh swee dez-oh-lay, zhet-ay on tran duh mon-zhay kon tü ay a-reev-ay)
I'm sorry, I was in the middle of preparing dinner when you arrived so I was a bit distracted. (informal)	Je suis désolé / désolée, j'étais en train de préparer le dîner quand tu es arrivé / arrivée, alors j'étais un peu préoccupé / préoccupée. (zhuh swee dez-oh-lay, zhet-ay on tran duh pray-par-ay luh din-ay kon tü ay a-reev-ay a-law zhet-ay urn puh pray-ok-oo-pay)
I was in the middle of writing to you when my mother arrived. (informal)	J'étais en train de t'écrire quand ma mère est arrivée. (zhet-ay on tran duh tay kreer kon ma maire ay ta-reev-ay)
I was in the middle of leaving the house when you phoned me. (informal)	J'étais en train de partir de la maison quand tu m'as téléphoné. (zhet-ay on tran duh part-ear duh la may-zon kon tü ma tay-lay-fone-ay)

I was in the middle of calling you when your letter arrived. (informal)	J'étais en train de t'appeler quand ta lettre est arrivée. (zhet-ay on tran duh tap-lay kon ta let-ruh ay ta-reev-ay)
July	juillet (zhoo-ee-ay)
in July	en juillet (on zhoo-ee-ay)
I visited Paris in July / I have visited Paris in July / I did visit Paris in July.	J'ai visité Paris en juillet. (zhay visit-ay pa-ree on zhoo-ee-ay)
I'm planning to visit Paris in July.	J'ai l'intention de visiter Paris en juillet. (zhay lon-ton-syon duh visit-ay pa-ree on zhoo-ee-ay)
I'm moving	Je déménage (zhuh day-may-nazh)
I'm moving to France in September.	Je déménage en France en septembre. (zhuh day-may-nazh on fronce on sep-tom-bruh)
because of	à cause de… (a koze duh)
because of you (formal)	à cause de vous (a koze duh voo)
because of you (informal)	à cause de toi (a koze duh twah)
thanks to	grâce à… (gras a)
Thanks to me!	Grâce à moi ! (gras a mwah)
Thanks to you! (formal)	Grâce à vous ! (gras a voo)
Thanks to you! (informal)	Grâce à toi ! (gras a twah)
I'm moving to France in July because of you! (informal)	Je déménage en France en juillet à cause de toi ! (zhuh day-may-nazh on fronce on zhoo-ee-ay a koze duh twah)
Do you want? (formal)	Voulez-vous? (voo-lay voo)
Do you want to prepare the dinner this evening? (formal)	Voulez-vous préparer le dîner ce soir ? (voo-lay voo pray-par-ay luh din-ay sir swar)
Do you want to eat something? (formal)	Voulez-vous manger quelque chose ? (voo-lay voo mon-zhay kel-kuh shows)
You want (formal)	Vous voulez (voo voo-lay)
to say	dire (dear)

You mean (formal)	**Vous voulez dire** (voo voolay dear)
I'm moving to France in July because of you! (formal)	**Je déménage en France en juillet à cause de vous !** (zhuh day-may-nazh on fronce on zhoo-ee-ay a koze duh voo)
Because of me? You mean *thanks to me*! (formal)	**À cause de moi ? Vous voulez dire *grâce* à moi !** (a koze duh mwah voo voolay dear gras a mwah)
Actually, I'm moving to Belgium too.	**En fait, je déménage en Belgique aussi.** (on fay, zhuh day-may-nazh on bell-zheek oh-see)
Actually, I'm moving to France next month.	**En fait, je déménage en France le mois prochain.** (on fay, zhuh day-may-nazh on fronce luh mwoire pro-shan)
Actually, I'm going to Paris next year.	**En fait, je vais à Paris l'année prochaine.** (on fay, zhuh vay a pa-ree lan-ay proe-shen)
a ticket	**un billet** (urn bee-yay)
wow	**ouahou** (wow)
thanks	**merci** (mare-see)
Let's go!	**Allons-y !** (a-lon-zee)
You need help, Louis / Louise! The Eurostar is fantastic and I was just about to book a ticket when you arrived. (informal)	**Tu as besoin d'aide, Louis / Louise ! L'Eurostar est fantastique et j'étais sur le point de réserver un billet quand tu es arrivé / arrivée.** (tü a burz-won daid loo-ee / loo-eez. luh-roe-star ay fon-tass-teek ay zhet-ay soor luh pwan duh ray-zurv-ay urn bee-yay kon tü ay a-reev-ay)
Oh, sorry. Actually, I feel like visiting Paris too.	**Oh, désolé / désolée. En fait, j'ai envie de visiter Paris aussi.** (oh dez-oh-lay. on fay zhay on-vee duh visit-ay pa-ree oh-see)

| Yes, when you talk about Paris you're so enthusiastic. | Oui, quand tu parles de Paris tu es tellement enthousiaste. (wee, kon tü parl duh pa-ree tü ay tell-mon on-tooze-ee-ast) |
| Wow, thanks! Let's go! | Ouahou, merci ! Allons-y ! (wow mare-see. a-lon-zee) |

If you've got through this without making any mistakes, then you're ready to read the final tip between chapters, which will tell you what to do next.

Well done for getting this far! Well done indeed…

Between Chapters Tip!

What to do next

Well, here you are at the end of the final chapter. You have worked hard and yet a different journey now lies ahead of you.

The questions you should be asking, of course, are: "what is that journey exactly?" and "where do I go from here?"

Where do you go first?

Well, that will depend to some degree on what you already knew when you began working through this book.

If you *have* found this book useful, then I would recommend moving on to my audio course, entitled "Learn French with Paul Noble". It uses the same method as this book except that you listen to it rather than read it. It will help to develop your understanding of how to structure French sentences and use French tenses still further, while at the same time gently expanding your vocabulary. In addition to that, the course will teach you plenty of tricks that will allow you to make rapid progress.

And after that?

Once you have completed the audio course, I then recommend that you use what I have at different times called "The Frasier Method", "The Game of Thrones Method", "The Buffy the Vampire Slayer Method" and "The Friends Method" – but the name isn't too important.

What is important is how the method works, which is like this...

Once you have gained a functional vocabulary and understanding of structures and tenses (from having used both this book and my audio course), I recommend that you then purchase an *English* language television series – a long one. It should ideally have something like 50 episodes or more (100 is even better). And it should also be something that you have watched previously.

This might seem an odd way to learn French but it's not. Trust me. It is in fact a very easy and enjoyable way to develop your ability in the language. I'm now going to explain to you exactly how this method works.

Almost all major, successful, long-running English language TV series will be available with a French dub. Typically, the version you can buy locally will have the ability to switch the language to French, if not you can go online and order the French dubbed version from there.

What you're going to do with the series you've chosen is to watch it in French. You should watch one episode at a time, whenever it's convenient for you to do so. And, when you watch it, you're not only going to watch it dubbed into French but you're also going to put on the *French* subtitles. If you use the English subtitles, you will spend your whole time reading them and will learn **nothing**.

Now while you watch the French dub of the series you've chosen, I want you to keep a pen and notepad handy and, when you hear a word you're not familiar with, I want you to write it down. Do this with the first twenty words you don't recognise. Once you've written those twenty down, don't bother writing any more for the rest of the episode. Instead, all I want you to do is to put a tick beside each of those words every time you hear them during the rest of that same episode.

When the episode is finished, take a look at how many ticks each word has. Any word with more than three ticks by the side of it is something you need to learn. So, look it up in a dictionary and then write it beside the English word in your notepad. Once you have a translation for each, use the checklist technique you utilised in the book to go through them until you can remember roughly what each word means. Then let yourself forget about them.

The following day, repeat this whole process again during the next episode. Something you'll begin to notice very quickly, however, is that those words that came up a lot in the first episode will also come up a lot in the second. This is because, on the one hand, any words that came up a lot the first day are likely to be quite important words anyway and, on the other, because you're watching a TV series, the same themes are typically repeated in different episodes. So, if you like *Game of Thrones*, you're going to very quickly learn the words for things such as "castle", "horse" and "wench". If you like *Friends* then you're going to very quickly learn the words for things like "coffee shop", "girlfriend" and "breakup".

And it's precisely because these same themes and the same language come up again and again that watching a long series becomes much more valuable than simply watching something like French films, for example. Were you to watch French films instead, you would quickly find that each film would almost certainly have a different theme and therefore the vocabulary would not repeat itself so much. When you watch a TV series, however, because you're looking up the most important vocabulary and because it's repeated in the series again and again, you really do end up remembering it. It becomes extremely familiar to you.

Now, you may say to this "okay, fair enough, but why does it have to be an English language series dubbed into French rather than simply a French one? And why should it be something I've seen before in English, why not something totally new"? The reason for this is simple: you will learn far more vocabulary, far more quickly, doing it this way. And why? Well, because if you decide to watch a French TV series, instead of an English one, you will immediately encounter unfamiliar cultural issues – the way people live, where they do their shopping, what they cook – much of this will be different. This means that, if you watch a French series, you will not only be trying to figure out what something means linguistically but, also very frequently, what something means culturally. It will simply present another set of barriers to your understanding, which is why it's best *to begin* with something familiar.

This leads us on to why it should be a series that you've already watched in English before. For the exact same reasons given a moment ago, you should also try to choose a TV series you've watched before because you will already be familiar with the context of the story. This will make it far easier to grasp what is being said, to catch words, to get the jokes and to increase your understanding more rapidly. Often, you will find that you can actually guess what a particular word means because you are already familiar with the context and this will make it far easier to pick up that word in French.

So, once you're finished with this book and my audio course (you will need to have done both to be ready to use this "Game of Thrones Method") go and watch a TV series. Keep a pen and notepad handy and use it in *exactly* the way I've described above.

If you do this, both you and your French will soar!

Good Luck – Bonne Chance !

PRONUNCIATION
GUIDE

Guide to the pronunciation of individual letters

In case you're still struggling with any of the trickier French words and sounds, I'm providing you with another additional resource below, which should make pronouncing even the most peculiar-sounding French words easy peasy.

Forvo

One wonderful resource that should help you with the pronunciation of more or less any French word is Forvo.

Forvo is a free service, which also requires no membership and no logins, where thousands of native speaker volunteers have recorded themselves saying various words from their languages.

If you're not sure whether you've got the pronunciation of a word quite right and it's worrying you, then simply go to forvo.com and type in that word. Frequently, you will find that the word has been recorded by several different people and so you can listen to multiple examples of the word until you feel confident that you know how to pronounce it.

So, if in doubt, go to forvo.com and have a listen!

A guide to pronunciation is provided under every word and sentence in this book. However, if you want some additional guidance on how to pronounce the trickier sounds in French, you will find below some help regarding how to pronounce French words when you see them written down.

Just take a look at the letters below to find how they are typically pronounced in French:

j is pronounced like the "s" in the middle of the English words "pleasure" and "leisure".

g before an "i" or "e" is also pronounced like the "s" in the middle of the English words "pleasure" and "leisure".

g before an "a", "o" or "u", however, is pronounced like the "g" in the English words "gun" and "game"

h is silent in French.

th is pronounced like the "t" in the English words "tap" and "table" (French has no "th" sound, such as exists in the English words "thing" and "thunder", for example. You simply won't find the sound anywhere in French, so don't use it!)

c before an "i" or "e" is pronounced like the "s" in the English words "sit" and "sand".

ç is also pronounced like the "s" in the English words "sit" and "sand" – but it is *always* pronounced like this, regardless of what letters it goes in front of.

c before any letters other than "i" or "e" is pronounced like the "c" in the English words "cup" and "coin".

ch is pronounced like the English "sh" – like in the English words "shoe" and "ship".

As for the vowels:

a and **à** are normally pronounced like the "a" in father.

e is normally pronounced like the "e" in verb.

é is normally pronounced like the "é" in café.

è is normally pronounced like the "e" in "get".

i is normally pronounced like the "i" in "machine".

o is normally pronounced like the "o" in "no".

u is pronounced by rounding your lips as though you are going to whistle but then, instead of whistling, keep your lips rounded and say "ee" (it will make a strange, unfamiliar sound, which is what you're looking for – well, it is French!)